W9-BAM-713

FLOWERS

FOR EVERYWHERE

CASTLE BOOKS

Photo credits

Harry Smith
Valerie Finnis
P. Genereux
Peter Hunt
K.A. Beckett
Violet Stevenson
R. J. Corbin
Iris Hardwick
Dennis Woodland
John Banks
D. C. Arminson
Ray Procter
Elsa M. Megson
Leslie Johns
C. Dawson
G. Hyde
D. Wildridge
Ianthe Ruthven
G. Rodway
Pamela Booth
P. Ayres
A. J. Huxley
R. J. Corbin
A. Rainbow
W. J. Tjaden
D. J. Kesby
Carlo Bevilacqua
Ruth Rutter
Amateur Gardening
H. R. Hood
J. E. Downward
Edna Knowles
Henry J. Wood
John Markham
John Hovell
Picturepoint
A. Boarder
Sheila J. Orme
F. W. Buglass
Mondadori Press
Tourist Photo Library
B. G. Furner
National Botanic Garden of South Africa
Maurice Nimmo
A. D. Schilling
T. R. M. Lothian
N. Chaffer
Slide Centre

CONTENTS

American edition reviewed and edited by Conrad B. Link, Professor of Horticulture, and Francis C. Stark, Professor and Chairman, Department of Horticulture, University of Maryland. The original of this book was published in Great Britain, primarily for British gardeners. The British flavor of this book is unmistakable, but the horticultural reviewers have endeavored to adapt the cultural and hardiness recommendations to the United States.

Copyright © 1974 Ottenheimer Publishers, Inc.
Copyright © 1968, 1970, 1973 Marshall Cavendish Ltd.
Printed in U.S.A. All Rights Reserved.

Modern methods and machinery have ensured that gardening
need not be a back breaking, or muscle-tiring job.
Here is a book which shows how — with minimum effort —
anyone can grow beautiful, fragrant flowers and give free
expression to their natural creativity.

People are creative. They transform a house into a home, furnishing it with comfort, decorating it with ornaments they choose, embroidering and embellishing it with the colors they favor. And this has always been so—even in the caves of primitive man. But today a garden — truly a frame for a well-run and beautiful home — is becoming more and more an extension of the home and people are tending to regard it as such. And so it is that rows of regimented scarlets, oranges and yellows are being quietly superseded by softer hues — by pinks, lavender, blue, grey, silver and even those kind, green flowers.

Handsome foliage, the furniture of the garden, is as much appreciated as the floral furnishings.

And today is a perfect age for the gardener since modern machinery and methods have taken much of the hard, muscle-tiring work out of gardening. Mowing the lawn, trimming the edges, clipping hedges, dull work, are often quickly done with the aid of electrical appliances.

The aim of most gardeners is to grow plants for beauty, for flowers to cut, f fragrance, for fun. They feel that a garden should be full of interest and delight, never demanding unending chores.

This book begins with the fundament advice on how to make gardens easy run as well as good to look at. Certai plants can serve the gardener as well as decorate the scene. It is important to know which to grow.

What most gardeners want most of all is to have something to admire, to wonder at, to cut, to look at from the house when they are busy within, a visual refreshment at all times of the year. This is possible and this book will help them decide what to grow and how to grow it. In their dreams, gardeners may see their homes wreathed in lovely undemanding climbers, honeysuckle over the windowsills, fences softened and even made beautiful by evergreen and floral drapes, unsightly sheds hidden by cascading blossom or a garage wall offering a home for fragrant roses. What is not generally appreciated is that by growing plants against any vertical surface, the area of actual garden is greatly increased, a practice which should be encouraged. Many climbers are both easy and spectacular. Some provide flowers for cutting.

One of the great maxims for gardeners used to be that for easy, successful gardening, one ought to stay with plants indigenous to the local area. Since soils vary considerably and since one can waste one's time and the life of a cherished plant by trying to force it to accept the wrong environment this seems good advice on the surface. But many gardeners on other soils envy those who garden on acid soil, who can color their plots with flamboyant rhododendrons and ground-covering heathers and other acid-loving plants, all of them requiring so little attention yet producing wonderful color effects, some of them even in mid-winter. I garden on lime soil yet I have all these plants by making special raised borders, using peat bricks as "walls" and more peat for planting. Anyone on any soil can grow peat-loving plants and so take full advantage of their amiable nature.

Meanwhile, of course, the main part of the garden can still be reserved for plants which are happy with the local soil conditions and climate.
Those who garden on limestone soils must decide well. There are many lovely plants which will grow splendidly in such gardens. Other problems to be dealt with are those of shade and seaside gardens, all of which have special plants to suit them.
Fortunately, there are scented flowers

and plants for every type of soil and since everyone loves these I have foun much to say about flowers for fragranc The garden should be an extension the house and what better link than patio distinctively and attractively furnished with plants leading from one the other? There is a great variety th can be grown successfully and prettily many kinds of containers. Many peop have "green fingers" and could easil coax and induce a mass of flowers fro a few plants — a potted flower show. This is yet another way in which one can increase the area of the garden, for baskets cascading with flowers and attractive foliage can hang overhead, windowsills can spill over with summer-long flowers and winter evergreens — greys or golds. There are sink and miniature gardens of many kinds for those who lose their hearts to the tiny doll's house proportions of alpine plants. Indoors, windowsill plants ensure some flower new every morning. About the home and for any room, there are longer-lived, evergreen plants, horticultural pets, which breathe life into the surroundings and provide companionship. You are never alone with a plant.

Flower arrangement gives one an opportunity to decorate the home with flair and at the same time it offers a medium of self-expression. If there is interest in this art, one will want to know what leaves, flowers, fruits and seedheads grow best; how to dry and preserve them for long-lasting winter arrangements; which are the most profitable plants to grow for cut-and-come-again flowers for spring and summer arrangements. All this information and more is here.

CHAPTER ONE
EASY GARDENING

One of the best ways of ensuring an informal garden is to choose plants which will work for you. The most important of these are known as ground covering plants. But ground covering plants bring out only the suppression of weeds and the conserving of moisture and fertility: they also are flowering plants in their own right, and contribute to the garden scene through the year, providing the lowly and diverse greenery that is needed to make effective contrast and texture to that of the shrubs. Even so, while they are mostly flowering plants, few of them flower for more than a few weeks and their foliage is, therefore, particularly valuable.

The perennials, evergreen (marked *) or deciduous fall into three categories: (a) those which spread freely by underground roots, (b) those which run freely on the surface, and (c) those which are clump forming, relying upon division for their increase. Examples:

(a) *Convallaria majalis, Asperula odorata, Cerastium tomentosum;*

(b) *Vinca minor* Stachys lanata, Tiarella cordifolia, Waldsteinia ternata*, Asarum europaeum*, Polygonum affine;*

(c) *Brunnera macrophylla,* epimedium, *Geranium macrorrhizum, G. renardii, G. ibericum platyphyllum, G. endressii,* pulmonaria, tellima*, *Stachys macrantha, Alchemilla mollis, Phlomis russelliana.*

In fact I have to begin with a word of warning. These plants are so ready to romp away that some have to be controlled.

Cerastium This genus has some undeniably attractive species with masses of small white flowers above a mat of grey leaves,

1 *Prunus pissardii* grown as a tree
2 The pink-flowered *Geranium dalmaticum*
3 *Geranium psilostemen, the most* startling magenta with black center
4. Here the golden leaves of *Lysimachia nummularia aurea* quickly spread over the surrounding paving stones
5 *Cerastium tomentosum,* called Snow-in-Summer because of the white flowers produced in June *on 6-in. stems. Easy to grow,* this is popular with new gardeners

but nearly all are very invasive and will romp anywhere in any soil, so caution should be exercised before introducing plants which may soon become weeds, in spite of their beauty. They are useful for covering difficult banks, particularly by a riverside, which are too steep for grass and need binding as a precaution against floods.

Also easy going are the many plants which grow in attractive masses both high and low and we shall learn more of these later. The following is an example.

Geranium (jer-ay-ne-um)
From the Greek *geranos,* a crane, because

Ferns make good ground covers in shady situations. For dry shade use Dryopteris felix mas and various polystichums. In moist situations plant Onoclea sensibilis

Ground covering plants suppress weeds and conserve moisture and fertility the seed pod resembles a crane's head and beak (*Geraniaceae*). Cranesbill. A genus of hardy herbaceous summer-flowering perennials with lobed or cut leaves, widely distributed over the temperate regions of the world. They are easily cultivated, free flowering, and some are useful rock garden plants, others good border plants.

Varieties of *Hedera helix*, the common ivy, are also good for shady banks, but take some years to create an impenetrable carpet. *Luzula maxima* is an ideal substitute for shady banks where grass mowing is difficult, and thrives best in cool, moist area. The most difficult positions to cover are found under big trees such as elms, beeches and cedars. Few plants will grow under the first two; but *Hedera helix* usually succeeds if the tree branches are high. A plant which will thrive in the same conditions is *Oxalis rosea*. For almost any position in sun or shade, on alkaline or light or heavy soils, *Hypericum calycinum* will be successful, while for really small borders many of the mat-forming rock plants are without peer, such as *Dryas sundermannii*, antennaria, acaena, cotula, ajuga, "mossy" saxifrages, *Hypericum rhodopaeum*, and many of these are suitable with the smaller spring flowering bulbs.

If you are interested in flower arrangement you will find many of these plant useful.

Alchemilla, for instance, is a great favorite When grown on the rock garden, it is bes planted in crevices between rocks. *A. mollis* 12 in., attractive, with kidney-shaped wavy-edged, softly hairy leaves and greenish-yellow flowers, good for cutting Contrasts well when grown in association with *Campanula poscharskyana*. Inclined to be invasive when established, but wel worth growing, especially as ground cove in shady or semi-shady places, such a: under trees.

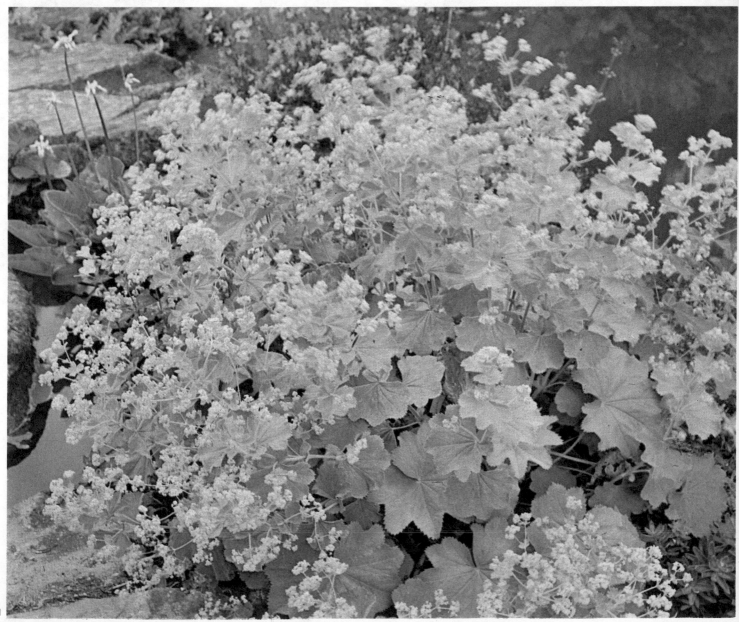

1

Alchemilla flowers will dry well for winter decorations. Cut the flowers when they are just mature, hang head down in small bunches in a warm, dark place until dry

If you like butterflies in the garden, plant Sedum spectabile, which they visit for the nectar of its late-blooming flowers

This is just one of many lovely foliage plants which are easy to grow.

Although green predominates, many plants have beautifully shaped or marked leaves. *Acanthus spinosus*, for instance, has leaves about 1 ft. in length, deeply divided and spiny and a deep, steely green that is almost grey. Some plants, such as the ivies, provide two different kinds of foliage, one on the young plant and also the mature foliage. In *Alchemilla mollis*, the lady's mantle, and its dainty relative *A. alpina*, the young leaves are pleated like a fan, and if sprayed with water hold silver drops, as they are covered with downy hairs. The true geraniums (cranesbills) are all very eas-

1 *Alchemilla mollis*, the Lady's Mantle, bears delicate flowers and is a ground cover plant for shady situations
2 Cineraria, euphorbia and senecio make striking contrasts in this town garden
3 Island borders, an up-to-date idea, can be looked at from all sides
4 Spring in a garden when color is provided with wallflowers, violas and alpines easily grown on a retaining wall

3

2

4

ily grown; *Geranium phacum,* and *G. ibericum* (hairy as well) provide especially good foliage, while the leaves of *G. macrorrhizum* color well in the autumn. More perenninials, the backbone of all good gardens to provide good green leaves, are the hellebores, particularly the handsome *Helleborus* which provides formidably spined dark, glossy leaves all the year round.

For a waxy texture the fleshy oval leaves of *Sedum spectabile* are hard to rival. Woolly-leaved plants usually like the sun, so choose the sunniest spot to get the best results with the evergreen *Ballota pseudodictamnus* which makes whippy branches with small round woolly leaves along their length. *Olearia mollis,* an attractive daisy bush, and its larger relative, *O. semidentata,* both have truly white woolly leaves. Soft white foliage comes on *Santolina chamaecyparissus* and *S. neopolitana,* the cotton lavenders, particularly on the latter, and both make a good low dividing line between flower border and vegetable garden. Try also *Anaphalis triplinervis* and *A. margaritacea* for double value; they have grey-white leaves in soft sprays and white "everlasting" daisies.

The artemisias provide soft plumes of silvery foliage. *A. absinthium* is almost frothy

1 The dark purple flowers of *Geranium phasum*, Mourning Widow
2 Buxton's Blue is a fine variety of *Geranium wallichianum*
3 Raised beds can be made to grow any type of plant
4 Herbaceous borders composed of perennial plants provide color and interest. Staking can be reduced by planting self-supporting up-to-date cultivars

1

2

3

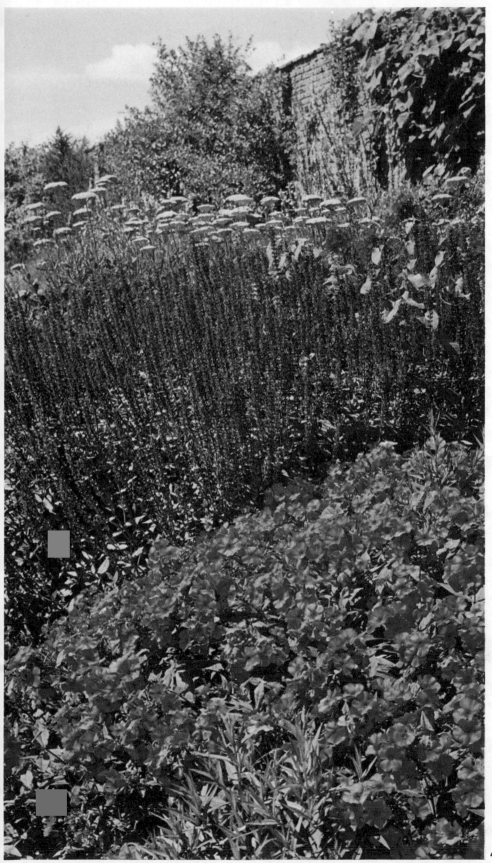

in effect, particularly the form "Lambrook Silver." *A ludoviciana* and *A.* "Silver Queen" both have good filigree foliage leaves which individually press beautifully. Among architectural plants par excellence for white woolly foliage are the biennial *Onopordon arabicum* up to 8-10 ft.

Although it is important to stake certain herbaceous perennials there are many others which are self-supporting, so choose these wherever possible. You might like to grow them in island borders.

If you like waist-high gardening, consider establishing raised beds in certain parts of the garden.

Paving stones, set in the ground on edge to form a square or rectangle filled with good soil, make delightful, small raised gardens where space is limited. Not only can the surface soil be filled with colorful plants, but the vertical space between the slabs offers an excellent site for trailing plants, such as alpine phlox, aubrietas, thymes, sempervivums (houseleeks) and various campanulas.

The top of the bed may be planted with unusual bulbs, such as those of South African origin which require very sharp drainage. Dwarf conifers and rare alpine plants which dislike winter wet may also be planted, and will be seen to better advantage.

Gardening for a small home

If you live in a cottage you can create a delightful garden to suit your home.

We cannot put the clock back, but there is no reason why the contemporary home garden should not reflect the old-world charm of its predecessors while making use, at the same time, of the new and improves varieties of older plants as well as some of those plants that have become more recently available.

Simplicity must always be the keynote of the well-designed cottage garden. This can be best achieved by a well-chosen mixture of suitable plants, by unpretentious design and accessories, and by the use of old-fashioned climbing plants to cover walls and fences.

Normally, the plants are so closely packed together that weeds get little opportunity to take hold. For the contemporary house, grass is almost certain to play an important part, but generally speaking, the lawn will be relatively small and it should be possible to maintain it in first-rate condition at all times.

4

Spring Spring is a season of major interest in the garden, beginning with the emergence of the snowdrops and winter aconites. The yellow buttercup-like flowers of the latter, with their attractive green ruffs, start to open during the first mild spells in January. Snowdrops, which come a little later, look best naturalized in grass. A position under old fruit trees — often to be found — suits them best. Both aconites and snowdrops seed freely if left undisturbed.

These will be closely followed by the early daffodils and many kinds of primula.

It would seem that almost any plant with the suffix "sweet" has affiliations with the cottage garden. Sweet peas, sweet williams, sweet sultan and sweet rocket are just a few of the flowers that have earned this name, probably because fragrance plays so important a part in determining the gardener's choice of plants.

Summer As spring progresses toward summer, the garden provides a continuous succession of color and fragrance. Wallflowers, often assuming their true perennial character and coming up year after year are followed by the sweet clove-scented dianthus — the cottage pinks and clove carnations.

Here again the present-day gardener has a much wider choice where the latter plants are concerned. Interest in the old pinks has revived and forms are now obtainable that flower continuously throughout the summer. "London Poppet" is white, tinged with pink and laced with ruby-red; "Laced Hero" has large white flowers laced with purple and a central eye of chocolate-brown.

Herbs Among the major attractions of the garden in summer are the fragrant herbs that provide material for sachets and *pot-pourris*, as well as for use in the kitchen. Lavender, of course, is the most widely grown of these.

A selection of herbaceous plants

Name	Height in feet	Color	Season
Acanthus	4–5	lilac-pink	July–Aug
Achillea spp & vars	1–4	white, yellow	June–Aug
Alchemilla	1–1½	yellow-green	June–July
Anaphalis	1–2	white	July–Sept
Aquilegia hybs	1–3	various	May–June
Armeria	1	pinks	June–July
Artemisia	3–5	grey foliage	Aug–Sept
Aster spp & vars	1–5	various	Aug–Oct
Astrantia	2–3	green-pink	June
Bergenia	1–1½	pinks, white	March–April
Campanula	1–4	blues, white	June–Aug
Centaurea	2–5	blues, yellow	June–Oct
Cimicifuga	2–4	creamy-white	July–Sept
Coreopsis	2–3	golden-yellow	June–Sept
Corydalis	1	yellow	May–Oct
Delphinium	3–8	blues, mauves	June–July
Dianthus	½–1½	various	May–June
Dicentra	1–2	pink	April–May
Doronicum	1–2½	yellow	March–April
Echinacea	2–3	purple-red	Aug–Sept
Echinops	2–5	steely blue	July–Aug
Erigeron hybs	1–2	blue, pink	June–Sept
Eryngium	2–4	glaucous blue	July–Aug
Euphorbia	1–3	yellow	April–June
Gaillardia hybs	2	yellow, orange	July–Aug
Galega	2–4	mauve	June–July
Gentiana	1–2	blues	July–Aug
Geranium	1–2½	pinks, mauves	June–Aug
Helenium	3–5	yellows, copper	July–Sept
Hemerocallis	2–3	yellow, orange	July–Sept
Heuchera hybs	1–2½	pinks, reds	May–Aug
Iris	1–5	various	May–June
Kniphofia	1½–4	yellow, orange	July–Sept
Lupin hybs	2–4	various	June
Lythrum	2–4	purple-red	June–Sept
Lysimachia	2–4	yellow, white	July–Sept
Macleaya	5–8	apricot pink	July–Sept
Malva	2–4	mauves, pinks	July
Monarda	2–4	various	June–Aug
Nepeta	1–2	blue	May–Sept
Paeonia spp & hybs	2–4	pink, red, white	May–June
Phlox	2–4	various	July–Sept
Pyrethrum	1–3	various	May–June
Salvia spp	2–5	mauves	June–Sept
Sidalcea hybs	2½–5	pinks	June–Aug
Verbascum	3–8	yellow, pink	July–Oct
Veronica spp & vars	1–3	blues, mauves	July–Oct

Perennials for cutting

Name	Height in feet	Color	Season
Acanthus mollis	4–5	lilac-pink	July–Aug
Achillea 'Moonshine'	2	sulphur-yellow	June–July
Alchemilla mollis	1–1½	yellowish-green	June–July
Anaphalis triplinervis	¾	white 'everlasting'	July–Aug
Aquilegia hybrids	up to 3	various	May–June
Aster (perennial)	up to 5	white, pinks, purples	Aug–Oct
Astrantia	2–3	greenish-white, pink	June
Coreopsis grandiflora	2–3	golden-yellow	June–Sep
Dianthus	½–1	various	May–June
Heuchera spp & varieties	2	pinks, reds	June–July
Iris germanica	up to 3	various	May–June
Phlox decussata	up to 3	various	July–Sep
Pyrethrum varieties	2	various	May–June
Trollius	2	yellow, gold	May–June

1 A garden made colorful with hollyhocks, dahlias and salvias
2 Part of a collection of herbaceous perennials, with a background of shrubs and trees
3 Bugle, helichrysum, stachys and houseleeks have a permanent foliage effect

CHAPTER TWO

A GARDEN FOR ALL SEASONS

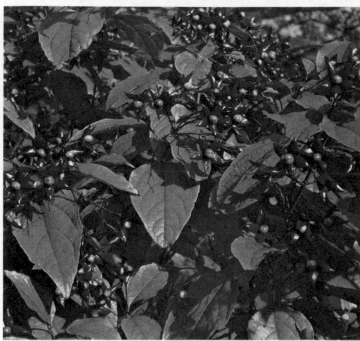

1 The lilacs, *Syringa vulgaris*, in a variety of color, are grown for their flowers
2 The berries of *Clerodendrum fargesii* are of a curious shape
3 Borders can be mixed or confined to plants producing flowers in varying shades of one color. This mainly yellow border is at its best in early summer when this color tends to predominate
4 *Cytisus scoparius buckwoodii*

Color planning your garden

Nature seldom, if ever, makes mistakes with color. Every hue seems to have full value and expression, not only to its own advantage, but also to that of the others surrounding it. Color clashes seldom occur in nature.

Foliage has as important a part to play as flowers in garden decoration; color variation in foliage is wide and of the utmost significance, vital to be borne in mind, especially where all-the-year-round decoration is the aim. Deciduous and evergreen leaves, therefore, should be allowed to play their full part, and not only through choice of plantings, but also by intelligent positioning in order to catch the sun in certain seasons, or to match and contrast with other plantings nearby.

This applies also to the wide and vivid range of ornamental berries and barks, so useful especially during the later and winter months, when blossom is scarce.

Winter, though always a little somber, sees many things in display; the sweetly scented *Viburnum fragrans*, *Chimonanthus praecox* and *Daphne mezereum*, as examples of some lovely shrubs. *Helleborus niger*, though sometimes wayward, will offer its sheer white "Christmas roses", the cheerful

winter aconites will shine, and snowdrops need no introduction.

Over all this, the conifers and evergreens in general maintain a perpetual source of attractiveness and interest if selected with a little imagination. And a special word must be said for the whole range of ericas, for here are species, hybrids and cultivars to provide blossoms of many forms and colors throughout the year.

Several factors come to bear when selecting planting material for a garden with the intention of providing as much color as possible. One of these is that of size and it is one of the most important. It should be remembered that sharp color contrasts are rendered more so in confined areas. Sometimes this is acceptable, but may also produce too bright an effect at close quarters; wiser, perhaps, to reduce the number of brilliant colors in small gardens unless adequate white is used to soften them.

Winter flowering shrubs By judicious planning and selection it should be possible to have shrubs in flower throughout the year. Winter-flowering shrubs make an individual contribution to our gardens, bringing color and, in many instances, fragrance during the darkest days of the season.

By mid-November, when the early heavy frosts have stripped the deciduous shrubs and trees of most of their leaves, the first pinkish-white flower clusters of *Viburnum fragrans* will be starting to open. This is one of the loveliest and most useful of winter shrubs; it continues to produce relays of richly fragrant blossoms right up to the end of February. There is a white variety, *candidissima*, with flowers lacking the pinkish tinge of the type, but which contrast even more effectively with the bare, cinnamon-brown twigs.

The witch hazels start to flower toward the end of January or early February. *Hamamelis mollis*, the Chinese species, with showy golden-yellow flowers — showy by

Red can be a difficult color to place. | White is a key color which stands on
Hues and tones are more effective | its own merits and acts as an
when distributed | incomparable foil

winter standards, at any rate — is the one
most widely grown. The form *brevipetala*
has shorter petals of orange, while those of
pallida are a pale sulphur-yellow.

   H. japanica comes into flower a little later;
the blooms of this species are more striking,
their golden-yellow strap-like petals being
set off by a purple calyx. They lack, however, much of the scent of the *mollis* varieties.

   More fragrant still is the winter sweet,
Chimonanthus praecox, with waxy, pale yel-

low flowers, the centers blotched with purple. In the variety *grandiflorus* they are of a pure clear yellow. The plant type starts to bloom in December or January.

February will see the bare branches of the mezereon, *Daphne mezereum,* covered in purple, hyacinth-scented blossom. This is a short-lived shrub and might well qualify to fill gaps in the border if it did not make such a valuable winter contribution to the garden. Fortunately, fresh supplies come easily from seed, and provided the scarlet fruits — which, incidentally, are extremely poisonous — are protected from the birds, which are very partial to them, the task of providing replacements is a simple one as the seed will germinate freely in any good garden soil.

From spring to summer the main display starts with shrubs such as the viburnums, brooms and lilacs and reaches its zenith at midsummer.

With the many plants to choose from, planning and planting for continuity of display should be easy. To obtain a lavish display of blossom for as long as possible it will be necessary to include in the planting plan shrubs such as *Caryopteris incana,* and the tree hollyhock, *Hibiscus syriacus,* the flowering season of which covers the months of late summer and autumn.

Lilacs rank among the favorite shrubs of late spring and the most decorative are the hybrids of *Syringa vulgaris*. Among both singles and doubles, old favorites still reign supreme, with "Souvenir de Louis Spath" as the best purple and "Maud Notcutt" most popular as the most outstanding single white. Lesser known single forms include "Esther Staley", and unusual shade of pale lilac vergining on pink, and "Maurice Barnes", the best examples of the true "lilac" color.

Many prefer the doubles with their "chunky", tightly packed conical flower trusses, although they lack some of the elegant form of the singles. "Katherine Havemeyer" (soft mauve), "Madame Lemoine" (white) are all established favorites. All of them, both single and double, have the typical enchanting perfume lilacs and are vigorous shrubs, reaching height of 15-20 ft.

In the smaller garden there will not much room for these giants, but some of th lilac species are much more compact an would prove useful where space is restricted. Their flowers may be smaller and less showy than those of the larger hybribut they yield nothing to these where frgrance is concerned. *Syringa macrophyl* for example, makes a dainty shrub, only 4 ft. in height, with elegant purple flow spikes that are extremely fragrant and ha an attractive habit of continuing to bloom intervals throughout the summer. *S. persalba,* a white-flowered form of the incorectly named "Persian" lilac is a delightf Chinese shrub with narrow leaves an handsome panicles of white flowers.

In late spring the shrub border is redole with fine perfumes. The mid-season vibunums, with their distinctive clove scent w be in bloom then; also *V. × burkwoodii,* vigorous cross between *V. carlesii* and *\

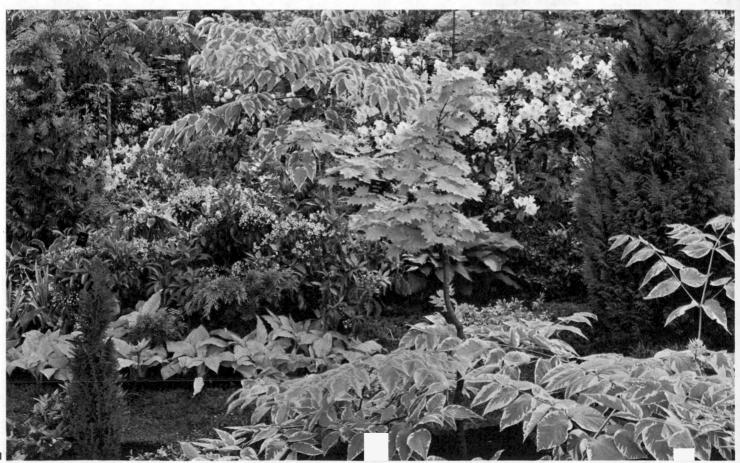

Calcifuges are lime-hating plants such as rhododendrons, camellias and aricas

To fill a garden quickly use some short-lived shrubs as stop gaps. Alternatively use the more ordinary kinds and remove them when the choicer kinds need more space

1 A border of mixed shrubs selected for either their flower or foliage color makes a decorative feature
2 Many shrubs are included in the garden for the brilliant color of their autumn foliage. *Fothergilla monticola* is one of these
3 Rhododendrons are among the most popular of spring flowering shrubs
4 *Garrya elliptica*, excellent in shade in mild climates

utile, with its large globes of white, *V. × carlcephalum*, another *carlesii* hybrid, with in this instance, *V. macrocephalum* as the other parent, whose large fragrant flowers measure 4-5 in. across and *V. carlesii* itself, still ranking as one of the most popular garden shrubs.

Midsummer beauty Philadelphus, or mock orange, often wrongly called syringa, will be among the next batch of favorites to come into flower. Its fragrance can be cloying and is too heavy for some tastes. The superb decorative value of their white flowers could never be in dispute. For the smaller gardens of today, there are a number of compact hybrids, much less coarse in habit than the once popular *P. coronarius*. "Enchantment" is one of the loveliest of these, with elegant, arching branches thickly festooned with double white flowers in June. "Manteau d'Hermine", only 4 ft. tall at maturity, also produces its double white blossoms freely. "Sybille", another shrub of modest dimensions, bears an abundance of dainty white, purple-scented blooms. *P. microphyllus* can be particularly recommended for the small garden. Its leaves are

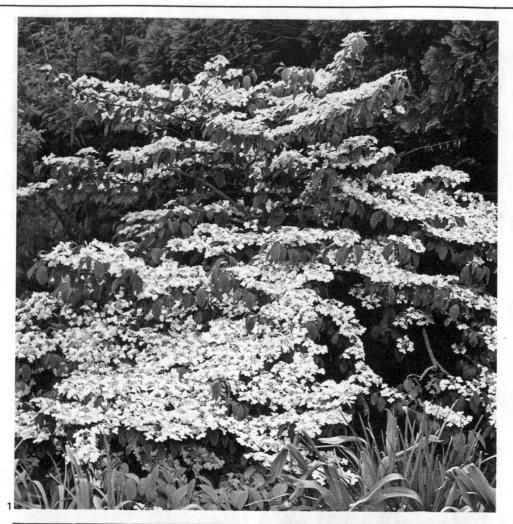

very small and the unusual four-petaled
flowers have a distinctive fruity perfume.

Weigelas, still listed sometimes as Dier
villa, are useful midsummer shrubs c
medium height and girth. Their flowers
borne along the entire length of the previ
ous year's shoots are long and tubular
rather like miniature foxgloves. *W. florida*,
native of Korea and northern China, wa
discovered by Robert Fortune in the garde
of a Chinese mandarin in the last century; i
is the hybrids of this attractive species tha
have produced our popular garden forms.

Cultivars "Eva Rathke" and "Bristc
Ruby" have flowers of a stronger color
"Eva Rathke" has the longest flowering
season. Its deep crimson flowers appear
from mid-May until August.

Deutzias, shrubs that deserve wider rec
ognition, will also be in flower at thi
period. Their habit of growth, narrow at the
base but arching elegantly outward whe
they attain a height of 4-5 ft., makes then
invaluable where ground space is at a pre
mium. The flowers, which are like smal
tassels, are profusely borne, while in winte
the bare branches are of great decorativ
value. *D. elegantissima* is the form mos
commonly encountered. The pinkish
purple blossoms are profusely borne or
arching sprays.

No shrub garden would be complete
without the summer-flowering viburnums
The snowball bush, *V. opulus sterile*, is the
most popular of these. Its globular flowers
green at first, but turning pure white later
make an established specimen of this lovel
summer shrub an unforgettable sight when
the branches are smothered in white snow
balls. It is, however, rather a vigorous
grower for small gardens and for these *V
tomentosum plicatum* would be a more ap
propriate choice. This seldom exceeds 6-
ft. in height and the "snowballs" are in the
form of half-globes which are borne in
symmetrical pairs along the branches, giv
ing the effect of a stylized Chinese scrol
painting.

Continuity of display In the rather barren
weeks that follow the peak flowering
period, hydrangeas are a standby. Apar
from the large-leaved species, which re
quire partial shade, they will thrive either in
full sun or semi-shade. In the former posi
tion, however, copious watering or regula
mulching will be required during the firs
few seasons after planting. *H. macrophylla* is
the well-known and deservedly popula

1

2

3

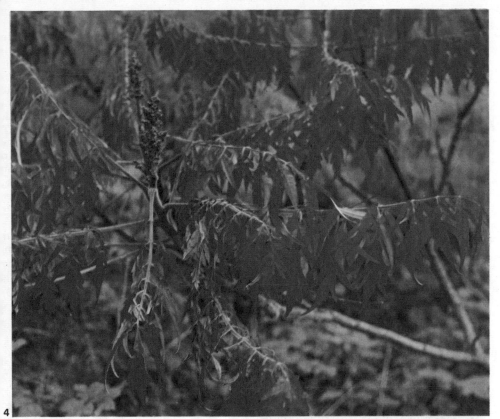

1 *Viburnum plicatum tomentosum* has its horizontal branches covered in creamy-white flowers in May or June
2 Red berries of *Vibrunum hupehense*
3 One of the plants grown for its bold red berries is *Skimmia japonica*
4 The feathery foliage of *Rhus typhina laciniata* colors well in autumn
5 The azara species are good shrubs in mild climates or a cool greenhouse. *Azara lanceolata* has bright yellow double flowers

pot hydrangea of the florists' shops. It will also do well out of doors in most mild climates, although in exposed positions the blossom buds, which begin to swell very early in the year, may suffer frost damage. In really cold areas it would be safer to plant one of the completely hardy species such as *H. paniculata, H. serrata* or the oak-leaved hydrangea, *H. quercifolia*.

Another genus of late-flowering shrubs, useful for bridging the gap between the summer and the beauties of autumn leaf color, is represented by the hypericums, or St John's worts, of which, the best known member is the prolific, *H. calycinum*. For the shrub border, however, the taller species and hybrids are a good deal more useful and decorative. Their flowers, like giant buttercups with a central boss of contrast-

ing stamens, make them among the finest shrubs for a late summer display. "Hidcote" and "Gold Cup" are both outstanding forms of *H. patulum*, with large cup-shaped flowers 2-2½ in. across. *H. elatum* "Elstead" is another attractive form, with oval leaves of a fresh vernal green, and masses of small yellow flowers in July and August that are followed by scarlet fruits.

To wind up the floral display for the season there is the so-called shrub hollyhock, *Hibiscus syriacus,* together with the blue-flowered *Caryopteris incana,* which is best treated as a herbaceous perennial and cut back almost to ground level each spring.

Shrubs for autumn leaf color The beauty of the shrub border is not restricted to its floral display. From September until final leaf fall comes a brilliant cavalcade of colored foliage, followed by—and sometimes simultaneous with—beauty of winter berry and bark.

Among the shrubs the leaves of which color so brilliantly, the barberries and cotoneasters play a prominent part. *Berberis thunbergii* has small leaves of a clear green that produce brilliant red in autumn. The leaves of the variety *atropurpurea,* which are deep purple throughout the summer, assume even more dazzling colors before they fall. *B. verruculosa* is an evergreen species, but many of its dark green leaves turn scarlet, while some of the foliage of the closely related *Mahonia aquifolium,* another evergreen, turns coppery-red in autumn and winter.

Although botanically the cut-leaved Japanese maples are not shrubs but small trees, they have so many of the characteristics of the former that they are usually included in this category.

The Japanese maples are very slow growers and the purple-leaved *Acer palmatum dissectum atropurpureum* and its green-leaved counterpart, *palmatifidum,* both with leaves like the finest lace, never exceed 8-10ft. in height. The leaves of the former turn a vivid deep scarlet, while those of the latter color to a lighter but no less distinctive hue.

Anyone who gardens on the moist, peaty soils in which rhododendrons and azaleas thrive ought to find room for *Enkianthus campanulatus,* which enjoys similar conditions and puts on a spectacular autumn display in orange and red. The Ghent azaleas, too, can be very colorful in autumn, as also can the common yellow *Rhododendron pon-*

ticum, when its sage-green leaves burst into tints of flame and coral.

One of the most unusual and striking shrubs for autumn color is a member of the euonymus genus, of which the spindle tree is probably the most representative. *E. alatus* has leaves that turn a bright glowing pink. After they fall, continuing winter interest is provided by the curious corky wing-like growth on the stems.

All the cotinus and rhus, related genera, are noted for their brilliant autumn color. The stag's horn sumac, *R. typhina laciniata*, is particularly spectacular, but this small tree colors rather early for the main autumn display and the display itself is somewhat short-lived. Much more satisfying are the brilliant orange and scarlets of *Cotinus americanus* or the bright yellow of the smoke bush, *Cotinus coggygria*.

Among wall shrubs and climbers many of the vines and creepers color magnificently, particularly the giant-leaved *Vitis coignetiae, Parthenocissus tricuspidata veitchii,* and the true Virginian Creeper, *Parthenocissus quinquefolia*. Where space is restricted, the smaller leaved and less rampant *Parthenocissus henryana* is useful for providing a wall tapestry of brilliant color.

On the ground, too, creeping and prostrate shrubs such as *Cotoneaster horizontalis, Gaultheria procumbens* and others will be putting down a red carpet, while the hypericums, that have only just finished their flowering season, will be adding to the autumn colors. *Hypericum patulum forrestii* has the most brilliant foliage of any of these.

Beauty of berry and bark Just as decorative, but with a longer lasting effect are the berries of many shrubs. These will continue the display from leaf fall until the New York —sometimes even later where birds are not numerous.

Once again, the barberries and cotoneasters are well in evidence, with species and varieties bearing fruits of many colors, ranging from the vivid coral red of *Berberis* ''Bountiful'' to the grape-purple of *B. darwinii*. Among the striking forms are *B.* ''Buccaneer'' and *B. thunbergii*, both with bright red berries and both, incidentally, also providing attractive leaf color. ''Cherry Ripe'' has fruits that are salmon-red and pear-shaped.

More than a dozen kinds of cotoneaster share this same valuable quality. The better known varieties include *C. horizontalis*, whose herring-bone set branches are

packed with scarlet berries and *C. simonsii*, a popular shrub for hedging and cover planting, with no less brilliant berries the size of peas. Taller forms and species include *C. frigidus* with clustered crimson fruits and *C. salicifolius*, the willow-leaved cotoneaster, that bears heavy crops of bright red fruits.

The pernettyas are a group of attracti small-leaved evergreen shrubs with show marble-size berries of an unusual beaut Not many of them, however, are se fertile, so that a specimen of the type plan *P. mucronata*, will have to be included cross-fertilize the more decoratively berrie forms.

The vacciniums, like the pernettyas, a ericaceous plants, and they include the ed ble swamp blueberry, *V. corymbosum*, ar others such as *V. macrocarpum*, the Amer can cranberry. *V. myrsinites*, the evergree blueberry, is native to southeastern Unite States.

Finally, to act as a background to th winter-flowering shrubs, there are oth plants whose main attraction lies in the strikingly colored bark or interesting branc formation.

1 The firethorn, *Pyracantha crenulata*, has red berries
2 The various forms of hibiscus produce flowers in August, a month in which few shrubs flower

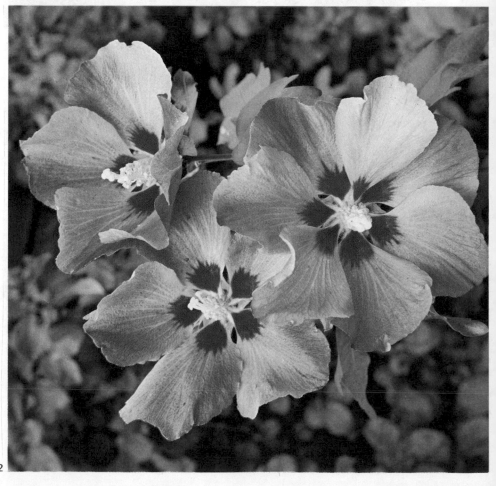

2

Certain shrubs are dioecious, with male and female flowers borne on separate plants. A specimen of each sex needs to be planted if there are to be berries

Some of the prostrate forms of cotoneaster make good ground covers. Cotoneaster dammeri and adpressus are examples

The dogwoods, both the scarlet and yellow-stemmed species, love moisture, while the curiously twisted stems and branches of *Corylus avellana contorta*, make an unusual and interesting tracery against winter skies.

Preparation of the site Just because shrubs *are* so easy to grow, it is a mistake to imagine that you can just stick them into a hole in the ground and then leave them to their own devices. Proper and careful planting is one of the most important operations contributing to their successful cultivation.

The initial preparation of the site should be done, whenever possible, a few months before planting is due to be carried out, in order to give the soil ample opportunity to settle. This may not always be possible, in which case a certain amount of raking and treading may be necessary on light sandy soils, while on heavier clays extra precautions will have to be taken to avoid leaving air pockets round the roots.

Deep and thorough cultivation, either by trenching or double digging, to break up the subsoil, as well as the top, is the ideal. Although the roots of the shrubs will eventually travel far, this preliminary cultivation will ensure that they get away to a good start in their first season.

Before the shrubs are put in, the surface soil should be broken up to a reasonably good tilth. Getting it into this condition will provide an opportunity of raking in a slow-acting fertilizer, applied at the rate of 3-4 ounces per square yard and should provide adequate reserves for the first growing season.

With a new garden, on former pasture or woodland, the chances are that the soil will already contain sufficient humus. First, the turf should be sliced off and placed at the bottom or, as far as woodland sites are concerned, all fallen leaves, leafmold, etc., should be collected and incorporated in the soil as digging progresses.

Where existing beds and borders are being given over to shrubs, it may be necessary to provide humus-forming materials in the form of sedge peat, leafmold, garden compost, or rotted straw, when the site is prepared.

Planting holes must be large enough and deep enough to accommodate the roots without bunching or overcrowding, and it is a good idea to leave a slight mound at the base of the hole on which the plant can rest while the roots are spread out and soil is worked among them. On light sandy soils this latter procedure will be simple, but with sticky clays, particularly if planting coincides with a wet spell, it may be necessary to fill in the holes with composted soil. Most shrubs will benefit by being planted in a mixture consisting of equal parts of sifted soil and peat or leafmold.

Depth of planting is important. The soil mark on the stem made at the nursery can be used as a guide and shrubs should be planted with the soil slightly above this to allow for the slight sinking that is likely to take place.

Normally, staking will not be necessary, although in positions exposed to strong winds it may be advisable to provide a temporary support for the first season to guard against root damage from wind movement. In any case, it is always advisable to go around newly planted shrubs after a spell of rough weather or prolonged frost to refirm the soil around the base.

Shrubs for specific purposes—climate permitting

For partly shaded situations

Acer japonicum (Japanese maple)
Aucuba japonica (spotted laurel)
Berberis (various) (barberry)
Buxus sempervirens (box)
Camellia
Chaisya ternata (Mexican orange)
Cotoneaster simonsii
Daphne mezereum (mezereon)
Garrya elliptica (silk tassel bush)
Genista (various) (broom)
Hedera (various) (ivy)
Hypericum (St John's wort)
Ilex (holly)
Kerria japonica (Jew's mallow)
Viburnum tinus (laurustinus)
Mahonia aquifolium (Oregon grape)
Pernettya
Pyracantha (firethorn)
Ruscus aculeatus (butcher's broom)
Sambucus nigra aurea (golden elder)
Vinca major and Vinca minor (periwinkle)

Foliage effects

Artemisia abrotanum (southernwood, lad's love)
Arundinaria and Phyllostachys (bamboo)
†*Cornus alba sibirica and C. alba variegata* (dogwood)
Cotinus coggygria (smoke bush)
†*Elaeagnus pungens variegata* (wood olive)
Euonymus alata
Hebe (shrubby veronica)

Hypericum patulum (St John's wort)
Laurus nobilis (sweet bay)
Pachysandra terminalis
Phlomis fruiticosa (Jerusalem sage)
Ribes americanum (American black currant)
Romneya coulteri (Californian tree poppy)
Rosmarinus officinalis (rosemary)
Ruta graveolens (rue)
Santolina chamaecyparissus (cotton lavender)
Senecio maritima
Sorbaria arborea
Spiraea arguta (bridal wreath)
Viburnum davidii
Vitis coignetiae
†*Weigela florida variegata*
*Good autumn leaf color
†Variegated foliage

Berried shrubs

Arbutus unedo (strawberry tree)
Aronia arbutifolia (red chokeberry)
Aucuba japonica (spotted laurel)
Berberis (various, barberry)
**Celastrus orbiculata* (climbing bittersweet)
Clerodendrum trichotomum
Gaultheria procumbens (partridge berry)
Hippophaë rhamnoides (sea buckthorn)
Ilex (various, holly)
Pernettya
**Pyracantha (firethorn)
Skimmia japonica
Symphoricarpos albus laevigatus (snowberry)
Vaccinium myrsinites (evergreen blueberry)

Viburnum (various)
**Wall shrubs

Shrubs for alkaline soil

Aesculus parviflora (bottlebrush buckeye)
Azara microphylla
Berberis (all) (barberry)
Buddleia davidii (butterfly bush)
Choisya ternata (Mexican orange)
Cistus (rock rose)
Cotinus (all)
Deutzia
Erica carnea, E. × darleyensis (heaths)
Escailonia (Chilean gum box)
Forsythia (golden bells)
Hibiscus syriacus
Syringa (all) (lilac)
Philadelphus (mock orange)
Potentilla (shrubby cinquefoil)
Rhus (all)
Spiraea (all)
Symphoricarpos (all) (snowberry)
Viburnum (all)

Waterside shrubs

Arundinaria, Phyllostachys (bamboo)
Cornus alba, C. stolonifera (dogwood)
Cortaderia (pampas grass)
Philadelphus (mock orange)
Sambucus (elder)
Viburnum opulus sterile (snowball tree)
Weigela

CHAPTER THREE
BEAUTIFUL CLIMBERS

These are the romantics of the garden. Everyone can find a place for at least one climber but the wise gardener will plant many more. House walls, garden walls, fences, archways, pergolas, trellises, poles, either single or erected tripod fashion, and other vertical or near-vertical features, provide the gardener with another dimension in which to grow plants. There are attractive plants available for this purpose, many of which benefit from the extra shelter provided by a wall or fence.

Types of plant Suitable plants include those which are true climbers, clinging to some form of support, either by tendrils (e.g. clematis), by twining stems (e.g. honeysuckles) and those known as self-clinging climbers, which adhere to their supports by aerial roots (e.g. the ivies) or by sucker-pads

(e.g. the Virginian creeper and some of its relations). In addition to these true climbers, there are many woody or semi-woody plants which are not, in fact, climbers but may be trained against walls. Examples of these are the well-known chaenomeles, climbing roses, ceanothus and certain cotoneasters.

An unusual way of growing certain climbers such as clematis or honeysuckles, is to let them clamber over dead trees or even up the trunks and into the branches of living trees. It is better to avoid for living trees the very vigorous climbers such as *Polygonum baldschuanicum,* although this is perfectly suitable for a dead tree, which it will quickly smother with its long, twining growths.

Some climbers may easily be grown in

1

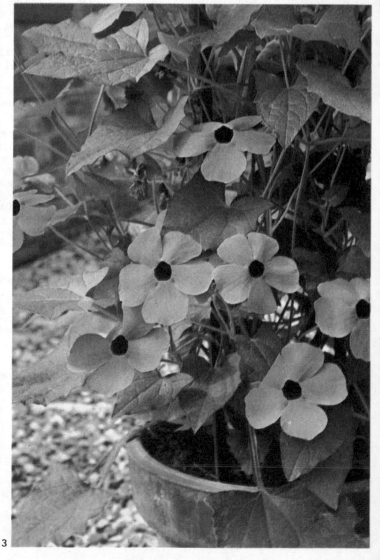

2

3

Plastic mesh and plastic trellis are non-rust, non-rot, easily fixed and always attractive

Never treat timber trellis with creosote. It kills plants

1 *Cobaea scandens*, a climbing
plant from South America
2 *Passiflora caerulea*, a beautiful
climber for warm walls
3 *Thunbergia alata*, Black-eyed
Susan, an annual
4 Morning Glory or Ipomoea,
an annual climber

well-drained tubs or other large containers and this method is useful where there is no soil bed near the wall, or in courtyards, patios or on town balconies.

Types of support Self-clinging climbers need little in the way of extra support except in their early stages. Once started they cling to walls, fences and the like, and need little more attention. Some gardeners are a little wary of the more vigorous self-clinging climbers such as ivies, but, provided they are not allowed to interfere with drain-pipes, guttering, roof tiles or slates, etc., they are unlikely to harm the wall itself. It can be argued that they help to keep the wall dry and the house insulated, by providing a leafy covering which keeps off even the heaviest rain.

Tendril climbers and twining climbers obviously need something to which to cling. In the open, garden poles, driven vertically into the ground or set tripod fashion, pergola posts and archways will provide support for twiners, but not for tendril climbers. These will need further support such as wire netting placed loosely around the poles to which the tendrils can cling. The growths of non-climbers will need tying-in to the support as they develop.

Against walls and fences there are various ways of providing support for plants. Trellis-work is a well-tried method and panels may be bought in various sizes.

Panels of plastic-covered, heavy-gauge wire netting are obtainable in various sizes, and these provide excellent support for plants. They may be fixed to the wall in much the same way as wooden trellis.

Wires, preferably covered, stretched across the face of a wall or fence, about an inch away from it, will also provide adequate support for many plants. However, unless the wire is properly strained it may sag in course of time. Vine eyes (drive-in pattern for walls, driven into the perpendicular jointing, screw-in type for wooden posts) are useful devices for fixing wires for climbing plants. Straining bolts, which can be tightened when necessary to take up any slack, are also obtainable. Lead-headed wall nails, nails with flexible lead tags, are used for individual ties, when it becomes

25

necessary to tie in long, woody growths such as those of climbing or rambler roses.

Flowering climbers on a house are so enchanting. The sweetly scented wisteria is a great favorite.

Cultivation Wisterias will grow in any ordinary well-drained soil. A sunny, sheltered position is essential. Provide adequate support for displaying the hanging "chains" to best advantage. Unnecessary vigorous shoots should be cut hard back in winter. Flowering takes place on short spur growths which should be encouraged.

Clematis (klem-a-tis or klem-ay-tis)

Clematis comprise the most useful and diverse group of shrubby climbing plants. The name is derived from the Greek *klema*, a vine branch, referring to their climbing habit. The large-flowered cultivars are showy and glamorous, and the smaller flowered species and hybrids are singularly adaptable and vigorous, and carry quantities of blossom. A wide selection of clematis may be had in flower from April until October.

All of them need some sort of support, unless they are being used as ground cover. On a wall, they will cling to lattice, wires or to other wall shrubs such as wisteria, pyracantha or roses. Most clematis will flower as freely on a north aspect as elsewhere. Perhaps they look their best when growing in the open over other shrubs, such as lilacs, viburnums and shrub roses. Or they can be trained, with the help of some wire netting, over tree stumps. They also make an effective vertical feature on a pole, arising from among lower shrubs or herbaceous plants.

2

1

Always keep clematis roots in the shade and flowers in the sun

Make sure your climber supports are strong and spreading before you plant; it will be too late when the plant is growing vigorously

Clematis in cultivation Most clematis are deciduous and very hardy. The few evergreen species need a sheltered wall for protection.
Pruning Methods of pruning of climbing clematis vary according to the season of flowering. They can be considered under three headings. (1) Early spring flowering. These include the small-flowered species *C. alpina, C. macropetala, C. armandii, C. montana, C. chrysocoma, C. spooneri* and all their varieties and cultivars. They need no regular pruning but if they become leggy or out of hand or are required to occupy only a small pace, they can have all their flowering trails removed *immediately after flowering.* (2) Early summerflowering, large-flowered cultivars, both single and double, that have already been considered as a group. It is perfectly natural for a good deal of flowering wood, in these, to die at the end of the growing season. All dead shoots should be removed in March when new growth is sufficiently advanced for live and dead to be easily distinguished. Thus, pruning consists in thinning out. (3) The species and large-flowered cultivars with a flowering season from late June onward should be cut hard back, annually, to within a foot or two of ground level. The safest time is March, but the plants look so unsightly in winter that many gardeners take a chance on pruning them in November, which is usually safe in a mild climate.

If you want your climbers to do really well and reward you handsomely, then you must ensure that they are planted properly. The site should be well dug and adequately drained where necessary.
Planting The footings of walls usually project several inches beyond the line of the

1 *Clematis montana rubens*
2 *Wisteria sinensis,* a favorite climbing plant, flowers in May
3 One of several forms of *Wisteria floribunda,* with long racemes of purple and white flowers
4 A tall shrub which is almost a climber, *Solanum crispum autumnale,* has showy purplish-blue flowers
5 *Clematis patens,* "Nellie Moser", flowers profusely in early summer
6 *Clematis florida sieboldii,* a striking and rare form. The center is composed of purple, petal-like stamens

wall itself and to avoid these and the drier soil at the base of the wall, the plant should not be closer to the foot of the wall than 6 in. Where there is enough room, a planting hole about 2 ft. wide and 1½-2 ft. deep should be made, to allow sufficient room for the roots to be spread out properly. If the soil is heavy clay it is better not to replace it but to use instead some specially made planting soil. The basis of this might be good loam, to which should be added generous quantities of garden compost and leafmold plus a handful of a complete fertilizer per barrow load.

Some temporary support should be provided for the plants until their growths reach the wire, trellis or other support and can begin to cling or twine. Even though this is temporary it should be firmly fixed to prevent the growths blowing about and being damaged. Short canes, twiggy sticks, strings or wires fixed to pegs driven into the ground, are all suitable.

Training and pruning Left to their own devices many climbers quickly become a tangled mass of growth, new shoots clinging to or twining around older ones, instead of neatly covering the supports provided and filling their allotted space. Some initial training may be needed to overcome this tendency. Such training consists in starting the new shoots off in the right direction and occasionally during the season ensuring that they are carrying on in the way they are desired to go. This is particularly necessary where it is required to train the shoots horizontally or nearly horizontally, since the natural growth of the plant is upward.

Shrubs trained flat against walls and fences usually need to have their vigorous wood removed from time to time. Very young growth developing from forward-pointing buds can often be rubbed out to prevent their development; otherwise the pruning shears will have to be used judiciously.

Pruning is often needed to keep plants under control or to ensure the production of new flowering growth.

Mulching An annual mulch around the bases of the plants, but not actually touching the stems, will help to prevent the soil from drying out in hot weather, particularly near walls and fences, will keep down weeds and will supply plant foods and improve the soil texture as the mulch is gradually absorbed into the soil by the action of worms and weather. Such a mulch might consist of garden compost, leafmold, par-

tially rotted leaves, or moist peat. Late spring is a suitable time to apply the mulch which should be several inches deep. The covering may be renewed from time to time during the summer.

Providing protection Some slightly tender plants may be grown successfully against walls in many parts of the country although in severe weather some protection may be necessary.

1 *Clematis macropetala* is a Chinese species
2 Hedera "Jubilee", a distinctive ivy with elegantly pointed variegated leaves
3 *C. jackmanii superba*
4 *Clematis jackmanii* "Comtesse de Bouchaud"
5 The climbing form of the rose "Caroline Testout" is ideal for a pergola

Climbers for Particular Purposes

Annual

Cobaea (P as A)	Ipomoea	
Cucurbita	Lathyrus	Tropaeolum
Humulus (P as A)	Pharbitis	Thunbergia

Greenhouse

Allamanda	Dolichos	Pentapterygium
Antigonon	Eccremocarpus	Petraea
Araujia	Ficus	Philodendron
Aristolochia	Gloriosa	Piper
Asparagus	Hedera	Plumbago
Bomarea	Hibbertia	Rhodochit
Bauhinia	Hoya	Rhoicissus
Beaumontia	Ipomoea	Smilax
Bougainvillea	Jasminum	Solanum
Cassia	Lapageria	Soilya
Cestrum	Metrosideros	Stephanotis
Cissus	Mikania	Streptosolen
Clerodendrum	Mitraria	Syngonium
Clianthus	Monstera	Thunbergia
Cobaea	Myrsiphyllum	Tibouchina
Colquhounia	Oxypetalum	Trachelosper-
Convolvulus	Parthenocissus	mum
Dipladenia	Passiflora	Tropaeolum

Tendril

Ampelopsis (D)	Lathyrus (D)	Passiflora (E)
Clematis (D & E)	Parthenocissus	Smilax (D & E)
	(D)	Vitis (D)

Twining

Actinidia (D)	Jasminum	Pueraria (D)
Akebia (SE)	(D & E)	Schizandra (D)
Araujia (E)	Kadsura (E)	Senecio (D)
Aristolochia (D)	Lardizabala (E)	Solanum (D)
Berberidopsis (E)	Lonicera (D & E)	Sollya (E)
Billardiera (E)	Mandevilla (D)	Stauntonia (E)
Calystegia (D)	Muehlenbeckia	Trachelospermum
Celastrus (D)	(D)	(E)
Holboellia (E)	Periploca (D)	Wistaria (D)
Humulus (D)	Polygonum (D)	

Walls north and east

Hedera (E)	Jasminum (D & E)
Hydrangea	Lonicera (D & E)
(D & E)	Vitis (D)

Shrubs, Wall plants (not true climbers)

Abelia (D & E)	Diplacus (D)	Phygelius (E)
Abutilon (D)	Forsythia (D)	Piptanthus (E)
Buddleia (D & E)	Hebe (E)	Pyracantha (E)
Ceanothus (D & E)	Hypericum	Ribes (D)
Ceratostigma (D)	(D & E)	Rosa (D & E)
Chaenomelas (D)	Indigofera (D)	Rubus (D)
Corokia (E)	Itea (D & E)	Schizandra (D)
Crinodendron (E)	Jasminum (D & E)	
Cotoneaster	Kerria (D)	
(D & E)	Magnolia (D & E)	

Note: For full details of the genera listed in these tables reference should be made to specific items in this book.

Key: D Deciduous. E Evergreen. P as A Perennial grown as annual. SE Semi-evergreen.

Large-flowered ramblers

Alberic Barbier	Creamy yellow
Albertine	Coppery pink
Breeze Hill	Straw yellow
Emily Gray	Yellow
Mary Wallace	Pink

Climbers of hybrid tea style

Climbing Etoile de Hollande	Hollande Dark crimson
Climbing Mme. Butterfly	Light pink
Climbing Mme. Caroline Testout	Pink
Climbing McGredy's Ivory	White
Climbing Mrs. Sam McGredy	Coppery red
Easlea's Golden Rambler	Yellow
Mme. Gregoire Staechelin	Deep pink
Paul's Lemon Pillar	Lemon white

Florbunda climbers

Climbing Allgold	Yellow
Coral Dawn	Coral pink
Dream Girl	Coppery salmon
Kassel	Coppery red
Parade	Crimson pink

CHAPTER FOUR
PLANTS FOR ACID SOILS

The easiest way to keep plants happy is to plant them in a soil which suits them. Some soils are just plain ordinary and there are hundreds of plants that will grow happily in them so long as they have proper nourishment. Others have a high lime content or may be acid. There are plants for both extremes. You can make a limy soil more neutral by using peat as a deep annual mulch or by incorporating plenty of it into the topsoil.

Plants which dislike lime are those which will not grow in soil which has a pH value (the scale for measuring the acidity or alkalinity of the soil) of higher than 7.0, and some ericaceous types do best at pH 5.5 or lower. The reasons for this are complex, but briefly, in such a soil some mineral nutrients become less available to the plant, for example iron, magnesium or manganese. Consequently the plant suffers from one or more nutrient deficiencies: if iron is lacking, the tip leaves become pale, almost white, manganese deficiency shows as yellowing between the leaf veins, and so on. With some plants the trouble is even more marked in that the roots never develop at all

and the plant simply dies soon after planting.

It is not easy to grow acid-soil plants in alkaline soils, and they may never do as well as they would in acid soils, but it can be done.

There are one or two chemicals which can be added to the soil to help the plants take up the right nutrients.

The group of chemicals known as sequestrenes have been specially formulated to overcome the difficulty. Iron, magnesium, manganese and so on are present in these substances in such a form that, when mixed with water and added to the soil, they can easily be absorbed by the plant roots — thus the plant no longer suffers from a deficiency. They do not make an alkaline soil into an acid one.

Acid soil plants include the family *Ericaceae*, for instance most rhododendrons, azaleas and heathers (except *Erica carnea*). Others are camellias, *Cornus kousa* and C. *sinensis*, halesias, liquidambars, some magnolias and styrax. Herbaceous plants and alpines, on the whole, are tolerant of lime, although lupins and *Lithospermum pros-*

tratum grow badly, if at all, in alkaline soils.

Peat beds

Acid-soil beds can be built on the ground level by using a low wall, 4—8 in., and filling the area with peat on an acid-soil—peat mixture. Logs may be used in a natural setting. The wall is not essential but prevents erosion. If the normal soil of the garden is an alkaline one, this allows you to grow many fine plants, especially among the *Ericaceae*, *Primulaceae* and *Pinaceae*, which you may otherwise have to forgo.

1 A path runs between borders richly planted with shrubs and perennials
2 Rhododendrons and brooms flourish to perfection
3 Hydrangeas will normally produce blue flowers only on acid soils
4 *Enkianthus campanulatus*, a shrub growing to 8 ft. that requires lime-free soil. Light shade is tolerated
5 Many plants will not grow properly, if at all, in alkaline soils.
Such plants include camellias

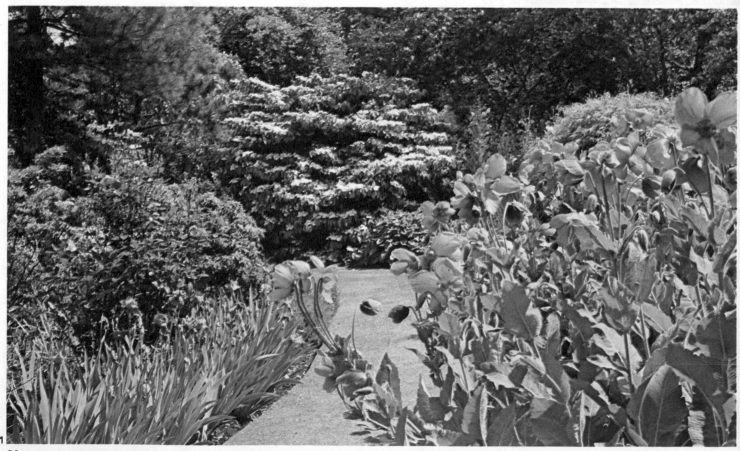

1

It is always wise to test the soil in your garden. Simple kits are available from garden stores

During the autumn months the whorls of the enkianthus leaves are beautifully colored

A semi-shady site is most suitable, such as below a tree or on the north side of a hedge or fence. If the soil is neutral fork it over first; if it is alkaline it is best to leave it but to lay down a 3—4-in. thick layer of rough peat before starting to build the wall.

Some of the most agreeable of the peat loving plants are the heathers. The majority are compact, dwarf-growing. Most species require a lime-free soil, although *Erica carnea* and its varieties, E. × *Darleyensis*, E. *mediterranea*, E. *terminalis* and the tree heath, *E. arborea*, are to a varying degree tolerant of alkaline soil. Hardy heaths are most effective and thrive better when grouped together than when dotted about singly. They are excellent plants for suppressing weeds. By making a careful selection it is possible to have heathers in flower in the garden almost throughout the year, provided there is sufficient space for a comprehensive collection.

The mountain laurel, *Kalmia*, are evergreen shrubs with dark, glossy leaves and exquisitely shaped waxy flowers. They thrive in an acid soil in dappled shade.

Rhododendron (ro-do-den-dron)

This is a large genus, with up to 600 species, ranging from prostrate alpine plants to tree-like specimens, some with enormous leaves. It includes those plants which were at one time described under the genus *Azalea* and others which were once included in the genus *Rhodora*. There are both evergreen and deciduous species and hybrids. One point which they have in common is that they will not tolerate lime in the soil, except for those mentioned below. The greatest number of species has been introduced from western China, Tibet, northwestern India and Burma; there are also a few from Java and Malaysia, which require warm greenhouse conditions. As there are probably well over 200 species and many hundreds of hybrids in cultivation, it is possible here to describe a selection only, under the main headings.

These are: *rhododendron section* species cultivated: hardy; tender; hybrids, hardy; *azalea section* species cultivated: hybrids, deciduous, mollis, Ghent, occidentalis, double mollis, double Ghent, Knap Hill and Exbury hybrids, evergreen hybrids. Those readers who require further details of species and hybrids in cultivation should refer to specialist works on the genus *Rhododendron* and to the catalogues of nurserymen who specialize in the genus.

Azalea section The first essential for azaleas is a lime-free soil and they grow best in a sandy loam containing plenty of leaf mold or peat, even a trace of clay, but they dislike a heavy wet soil or being baked dry at the roots in summer. They will flower well in full sun, provided that the roots remain reasonably moist and cool, and when grown in an open sunny position the colors are often more intense and the attractive bronze tint to the young leaves in spring is more pronounced, whereas in partial shade this may be absent. Nevertheless azaleas are admirable for a woodland garden in dappled shade and the trees not only provide a beautiful setting, but afford some protection to the blooms which may otherwise be damaged by late spring frosts.

Azaleas associate well with maples *(acers)*, hardy heathers, kalmias, enkianthus and small-growing shrubs in the rhododendron section of the genus, all of which thrive in an acid or lime-free, well-drained soil. The

1

2

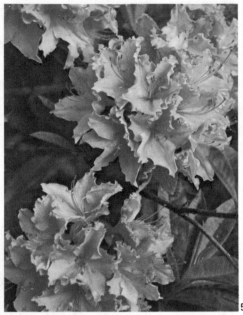

1 The tubular flowers of
Rhododendron keysii
2 *Erica vulgaris*
3 *Kalmia latifolia* "Brilliant" has full
heads of deep pink flowers
4 *Kalmia latifolia* is an evergreen
with waxy pink flowers
5 Exbury hybrid azaleas, such as
this apricot seedling, have been
evolved at the Exbury estate over
a long time

maximum effect is obtained by planting in groups, even of three, if space does not permit for more liberal planting. As they can be lifted with a good ball of soil attached to the roots, planting may be done at any time during the dormant season from late October to about mid-March. Well-budded young plants will usually flower quite happily the first season after being planted. A mulch each autumn of leaf mold, moist peat, or garden compost will keep the shrubs in good condition. Wood ash contains a high proportion of lime, and this should be used sparingly, if at all.

Deciduous hybrid azaleas

Hardy, hybrid azaleas are unsurpassed for brilliance and diversity of color in the spring and early summer. Autumn color of foliage is often splendid.

Mollis hybrids These grow 4–5 ft. tall, and bear large trusses of scentless flowers, of almost translucent texture, which start to

1

2

open in early May, before the leaves unfold.

Ghent hybrids These reach 6−8 ft. tall and have elegant, tubular, honesuckle-shaped fragrant flowers, which open in May when the leaves have developed.

Double Mollis and double Ghent hybrids These are 5−8 ft. tall, with fragrant flowers in May or June. Cultivars include "Aida", rose-pink with deeper flush; "Byron", white, tinged rose; "Norma", bright rose; "Phidias", cream, flushed rose.

Azalea occidentalis hybrids (*R. occidentale*) Plants in this group grow up to 10 ft. tall, and have large trusses of fragrant flowers from mid-May to early June, in delicate shades of pink, cream or white flushed with pink.

Knap Hill hybrids and Exbury hybrids These grow 4 - 8 ft. tall. They are two splendid strains which have been evolved over the years at the Knap Hill Nursery near Working, Surrey, and at the Rothschild's estate at Exbury, England. Leading nurserymen offer numerous named cultivars as well as plants raised from seed collected from selected, outstanding plants. The flowers

3

4

are in shades of apricot, flame, pink, crimson, orange, yellow and cream, from early May to mid-June. Double-flowered varieties are also now available.

Evergreen hybrid azaleas

The heights of these range from 2−6 ft. They were mainly raised by plant breeders in Japan and in Europe. Some start to flower in April but the majority are at their best in

May when they are profusely covered with bloom.

Hardy hybrids These hybrids range from those of dwarf and medium habit, suitable for a small garden, to those which eventually develop into large shrubs suitable for a spacious woodland setting. The diversity of color and form of the individual flowers are remarkable.

When you make a peat wall it should be battered, i.e., sloped slightly backwards

Although peat is acid it is unlikely to make other soils appreciably more acid unless very large amounts are used regularly or a very acid peat is used

5

6

7

The hardy hybrid rhododenrons range from small shrubs to near trees in height
1 Rhododendron "Mermaid"
2 Rhododendron "Queen WILHELMINA"
3 Rhododendron "Susan" has mauve flowers
4 *Rhododendron quinquefolium*, from Japan, has broad, ball-shaped white flowers and deciduous pale green leaves
5 The lily-of-the-valley like flowers of *Arbutus unedo*, the Strawberry Tree
6 *Camellia sasanqua* is a winter-flowering Chinese species
7 Camellia "Donation"
8 Azaleas as well as most other members of the heather or erica family, like acid soils

Camellia

The value of the camellia as an outdoor evergreen flowering shrub, is not always fully appreciated; for long treated as tender, it is now taking its place with rhododendrons and azaleas among hardy shrubs. The leaves are dark glossy green, the flowers white, pink, or red, sometimes attractively striped, mostly borne in March and April (earlier under glass). Height varies according to conditions and can be 15 ft. or more. Plants have the advantage of flowering when very young, at only 1½ ft. These shrubs require a position sheltered from cold winds and early morning sun; it is the latter, causing a quick thaw which damages the blooms on frosty mornings. Light woodland or north-facing borders should be chosen.

8

CHAPTER FIVE

GARDENING ON CLAY SOILS

Gardening on clay can be a frustrating and disappointing business unless unless you are prepared to work hard to cultivate the soil before you attempt to plant it. Most clay soils are difficult to work but when properly managed are fertile and capable of supporting strong growth of a wide range of plants. Their nature varies according to the proportion of pure clay contained in them and when the amount is high the soil is badly drained, sticky and heavy with the large quantities of water they hold. The high content of water also delays their warming up in spring and because of this, early sowing and planting cannot begin until the season is well advanced. Draining is therefore a vital first step toward the improvement of some of these soils. While some may need elaborate drainage systems to bring about success, others may improve with systematic cultivation over a few years.

Virgin land with a high proportion of clay should be double dug when turning it over the first time. This is necessary to break up the hard layer of compacted soil a spade's depth down which so often prevents water escaping from the surface. Digging should be done in autumn and the top soil left in large lumps as deposited from the spade in order that alternate frosts and rain may help break it down into small crumbs ready for the preparation of seed beds in spring.

Small chips can be mixed into the soil at the bottom of the trench formed while double digging is being done and will help to keep the soil open. Manures, peat, weathered ashes and crushed clinker give similar benefit. Stones already in the soil should be left in as they will assist drainage.

Horse manure is the best kind to use on clay soils. This is because it is light, drier and less sticky than other animal manures. Near towns, horse manure is often obtainable from riding stables, but in areas where it cannot easily be obtained, compost may be used instead or the land may be seeded with quick growing crops such as mustard,

1 Philadelphus, mock orange, often erroneously called Syringa, will grow in clay soil. This is the double fragrant. "Virginal"
2 Viola "Maggie Mott" requiring good drainage
3 Crinum × powellii, for a south-facing well-drained border
4 Eremurus elwesii alba flowers in May on stems 6 - 9 ft. in height. A warm sunny position is advisable: clay soil is tolerated with an annual mulch

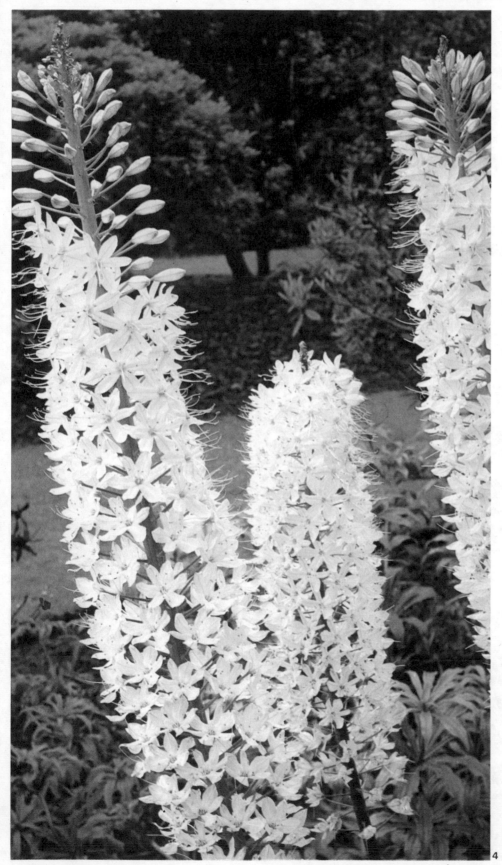

rape, or vetch which can be dug in as green manure before the flowering stage is reached.

Ridging may be necessary if the soil is very heavy and almost impossible to break down in spring. This method exposes a larger surface of soil to the action of the weather and to be fully effective it must be started in the autumn and the ground left rough throughout the winter. In spring, the soil should be leveled out and forked but no deeper than 4–6 in., otherwise wet soil from below is brought up to the surface and the purpose of the operation is spoiled. Substantial amounts of coarse sand, grit or horticultural grade peat may be worked in at the same time to improve the surface soil.

Lime is a valuable conditioner to use for improving the physical structure of all clay soils. It binds the small particles together into small crumbs, allowing water to pass into the sub-soil and air to dry out the top soil. It helps to convert soil chemicals into plant food, and accelerates the decomposition of organic material which is often slow rotting in clay. It also neutralizes acids which are often excessive and the cause of disease in this kind of soil.

Apply the lime after digging is finished. Ground limestone is a valuable form to use on the heaviest clays and should be applied at rates of 6–12 ounces per square yard. Lime should not be used within a month of manuring and after application should be mixed into the soil.

Certain fertilizers cause a marked deterioration in the structure and chemical state of clay soils. Sulphate of ammonia makes the soil more acid, while nitrate of soda can make the soil sticky and ruin its crumb structure by deflocculating the clay particles. Both sulphate of ammonia and nitrate of soda can be replaced by calcium nitrate which is applied either as a dressing before planting or for topdressing around plants in growth.

During hot weather in spring and summer large cracks appear in clay as it dries out and shrinks. Very often these cracks form along rows of small seedlings, probably because the amount of water taken up by them causes more rapid shrinkage of the soil in that area. To avoid this, the soil must be hoed regularly to keep the surface loose and prevent evaporation of water from just beneath the surface. Mulching with manure, compost, lawn mowings or black polyethylene will serve the same purpose.

Finally, keep off the soil if it is very wet. In

4

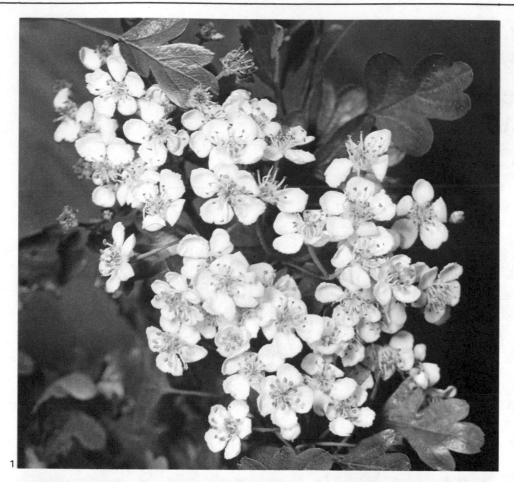

spring, try to start preparing seedbeds just before the soil dries out completely. Some clay soils become brick hard and almost impossible to break up when dry.

What peat does Like all humus suppliers, it makes soils more porous by giving them a kind of open structure by virtue of the millions of small cells that make up its fibrous structure. As a result, heavy soils are opened up and light soils hold more moisture for plant use. Peat is scattered in drills for vegetable crops, the seedlings are able to push their way through the more difficult

1 *Crataegus* × *lavallei,* a tree that can reach 20 ft. It is a hybrid raised about 1870 at the Jardin des Plantes, Paris
2 The attractive *C. oxyacantha paulii,* a double form
3 Kniphofia "springtime", typical of the Red Hot Pokers
4 The tangerine colored flowers of *Buddleia globosa*
5 *Buddleia davidii* is the most popular kind, known as the Butterfly Bush because its spikes of bloom in the late summer attract these insects
6 A modern aquilegia hybrid. Much of their beauty comes from the long spurs behind the flowers

soils, which form hard crusts during dry periods.

One of the reasons for the popularity of peat is the ease with which it is spread and mixed with the soil; it is also weed free, clean to handle and has a longlasting effect on the soil.

But always thoroughly moisten the peat first; never work it in dry — otherwise it will stay dry and fail to give the best results. If peat is to be used in quantity, one way of ensuring that it is properly moistened is to break up the bale, and either allow it to be soaked by rain or apply water with a sprinkler, which may take quite a time. Another way is to make a hole in the bale and insert the hose and allow water to trickle in gently until the bale is thoroughly soaked through. Even then it may be necessary to break up

the bale afterward and use the sprinkler to make sure that there are no dry patches left.

Smaller quantities can be moistened by soaking overnight in a bucket or other container, after breaking up the lumps by hand. The next day the excess water should be squeezed out before the peat is used.

For overcoming the harmful effects of crusting, scatter 3 ounces of peat per square yard when preparing seed rows. To help the roots of trees and shrubs to spread evenly through poorly structured soils, put 2–3 pounds of peat under each plant when planting shrubs, roses or fruit bushes; a handful is all that is needed for herbaceous plants. Always mix peat with a little loose soil before positioning the plant.

Mulches of peat help to keep shrub and flower borders free from weeds and the soil

6

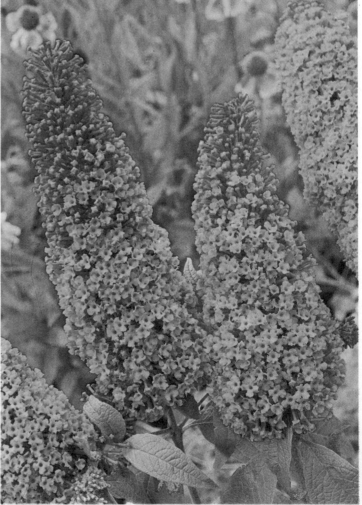

5

moist during the summer, after which the material can be worked into the soil. A 1/16—½ in. grade product, when applied at the rate of 6—10 pounds per square yard, is best for this work.

When preparing the soil for sowing lawn seed or laying sod, peat worked into the top 2 in. will give a good start to the germinating seeds or help the sod to knit together. A special grade peat is supplied for autumn dressing of lawns.

Peat pots are being increasingly used for seedlings and bedding plants. The pot is put into the soil, thus leaving the roots undisturbed. The roots penetrate the peat and finally it is broken down into the soil.

1

2

3

4

Cover bare soil with a deep layer of grass cuttings. As these decompose they will add humus to the soil

Good mulches of peat around roses will save hoeing and possibly prevent injuring the surface spots

5

8

1 *Campanula portenschlagiana,* a hardy trailing June flowering plant
2 *Contoneaster Conspicuus,* a wide-spreading shrub reaching 4 - 5 ft. in height
3 *Rosa damascena versicolor,* the "York and Lancaster" rose, was known prior to 1629. The flowers are pink or white or parti-colored but not striped as in *Rosa gallica versicolor* ("Rosa mundi")
4 *Rosa gallica versicolor.* "Rosa mundi", has grown since the sixteenth century, when it was first recorded
5 Hostas, plantain lilies
6 The berries of *Viburnun lantana* are first red, ripening to black
7 The ribbed leaves and deep blue berries of *Viburnum davidii*
8 *Viburnum opulus fructo-luteo,* the yellow-fruited form of the Guelder Rose, or Snowball Tree

6

7

Some Plants Suitable for Clay Soils

Achillea (HP)	Deutzia (S)	Jasminum (S)	Ribes (S)
Aconitum (HP)	Diervilla (S)	Juniperus (T)	Rudbeckia (HP)
Althaea (HP)	Digitalis (HBi/P)	Kerria (S)	Rhus (S)
Anchusa (HP)	Doronicum (HP)	Kniphofia (HP)	Robinia (S/T)
Anemone (HP)	Echinops (HP)	Laburnum (T)	Salix (T)
Aquilegia (HP)	Ericas (S)	Laurus (S/T)	Senecio (HP/S)
Aster (HP)	Escallonia (S)	Lonicera (S)	Skimmia (S)
Berberis (S)	Euonymus (S)	Lupinus (HP)	Solidago (HP)
Bergenia (HP)	Forsythia (S)	Lythrum (HP)	Sorbus (T)
Betula (T)	Galega (HP)	Mehonia (S)	Spiraea (S)
Buddleia (S)	Geranium (HP/RP)	Narcissus (Bu)	Symphoricarpos (S)
Buxus (S)	Geum (HP)	Nepeta (HP)	Syringa (S)
Campanula (HP/RP)	Hebe (S)	Papaver (HP)	Taxus (T)
Cercis (T)	Helenium (HP)	Philadelphus (S)	Thuja (T)
Chaenomeles (S)	Helianthus (HP)	Picea (T)	Tradescantia (HP)
Chamaecyparis (T)	Heliopsis (HP)	Potentilla (HP/S)	Trollius (HP)
Chrysanthemum (HP)	Helleborus (HP)	Primula (HP/RP)	Verbascum (HBi/P)
Cotinus (S)	Hemerocallis (HP)	Prunus (T)	Veronica (HP)
Cotoneaster (S)	Hydrangea (S)	Pyracantha (S)	Viburnum (S/T)
Crataegus (S/T)	Ilex (S/T)	Quercus (T)	Vinca (S)
Daphne (S)	Iris (HP)	Rosa (S)	Viola (HP)

Bi Biennial, **Bu** Bulb, **H** Herbaceous, **P** Perennial, **RP** Rock Plant, **S** Shrub, **T** Tree

Note: The great majority of plants, including vegetables and fruit, will grow successfully on clay soils; those listed above are merely a few of those which do exceptionally well.

CHAPTER SIX

GARDENING ON ALKALINE SOILS

1

Alkaline soils

So much is heard about the beauties of the rhododendrons, azaleas, pieris, summer-flowering heaths, stewartias and some of the magnolias that the gardener whose land is on limestone is left feeling rather deprived. There is, however, no need for disappointment. There are quite as many lovely, colorful, free-flowering and fruiting plants which will thrive in alkaline conditions as on acid soils and, provided that the gardener on alkaline soil is prepared to go to the trouble to understand the soil and to meet its problems.

Two main types of alkaline soils are to be found — the shallow soil overlying limestone rock and the heavy, sticky limy clay known as marl. In addition to these two naturally occurring alkaline soils one some-

1 A small enclosed garden Kent
2 *Geranium atlanticum*
3 *Scabiosa caucasica* "Sarah Cramphorn"
4 *Sempervivum*, the familiar houseleek
5 The Oriental poppy, *Papaver orientale*, of which there are many forms
6 *Agapanthus campanulatus*, the African Lily, flourishes at the base of a sunny wall in well-drained soil
7 Carnations are among the many plants that flourish on alkaline soils

2

The types of vegetation found growing on calcareous soils often differ tremendously and depend upon the depth of soil on top of the limestone

Some of the most easily worked soil is in areas where the limestone is some 2-3 ft. below the surface. It retains moisture and yet any excess is quickly drained

3

6

4

5

7

of manure) and allowed to stand for 1 year before use. An acid grade of peat, garden refuse composted and litter from poultry are also valuable. Where waterlogging occurs however, a drainage system is necessary and this should be provided before any attempt is made to treat the soil.

Light alkaline soils overlying limestone are "hungry", absorbing all added nutriment almost as quickly as it is added, thus being just as poor as before. On such soils it is necessary to add organic matter at every opportunity — the coarser the better, so as to slow down the process of decomposition. Animal manure, poultry manure composted with straw, peat, seaweed and leafmold from acid-soil areas all help. In addition every possible scrap of vegetable and animal waste should be composted, ready to be dug into the soil or added as a surface mulch.

times finds old vegetable gardens and similar sites which have a high alkalinity due to years of over-liming by their owners. These are best corrected by refraining from adding further lime and, instead, digging in quantities of acid material such as rotted leaves or poultry manure composted with baled straw built up in layers (4 in. of straw to 2 in.

Another difficulty to be encountered on these shallow alkaline soils is the lack of depth, and consequent drying out. This can be counteracted by excavating good individual holes for all permanent plants, breaking up the rock with a pick-axe to a fine rubble. This rubble then acts as a sponge, retaining moisture and giving a good hold to thirsty roots. Once plants get their roots down in this way they will grow strongly, often making exceptionally fine specimens.

Once the initial cultivation has been carried out, it remains to choose only those plants that succeed on alkaline soils. Little lasting satisfaction comes from struggling to grow acid-loving plants on alkaline soils. It is far better to stick to known lime-lovers and enjoy the glorious healthy growth which will succeed your efforts. One or two misapprehensions exist, however, over which plants are in fact lime-haters. The rugosa roses, these strong-growing, free-flowering, shrubby roses from Japan, have sometimes been listed among those that dislike lime. This is very far from the truth. These lovely and useful roses will grow in alkaline clay or even in almost pure sand made alkaline by the accumulated deposit of seashells. Such sites are often found in sandy patches near the shore. As a general rule it is those plants with the strongest root systems that do best in limestone soils. Hybrid tea roses of the "Peace" family, strong-growing floribundas such as "Queen Elizabeth", climbers such as the more vigorous H.T. sports: "Climbing Shot Silk", "Souvenir de Claudius Denoyal", and such strong growing ramblers as "Albertine", "Emily Gray", "Dorothy Perkins" and "Debutante" are ideal.

Among perennials, too, it is the stronger growers that do best. The plume poppy *Macleaya cordata*, paeonies of all kinds, asters, heleniums, pinks and carnations *Stachys lanata*, the stately eremuri, the graceful feathery *Spiraea aruncus* will all succeed, provided the underlying hard pan has been broken up. Sun lovers such as the artemisias with thei decorative silvery leaves

Although some geranium species will grow well on limestone soils others hate lime, so use plenty of peat when planting

The beautiful arbutus is one of the few trees of the erica or heather family which will grow on limestone soils

istus species, lavender, choisya, rosemary and elaeagnus do well on shallow, alkaline soils; the sharp drainage making them hardier than they are elsewhere. Among shrubs and trees; lilacs, philadelphus, sorbus species, cotoneasters and chaenomeles like alkaline soil. On limestone they flower and fruit abundantly and their autumn color is often magnificent. Clematis, too, are natural lovers of alkaline places, but the large-flowered kings need plenty of moist peat packed around their roots at planting time if they are to succeed. This technique gives wonderful results with dahlias, antirrhinums and petunias. Lupins and schizostylis are often said to be lime-haters but damp peat around their roots acts as a buffer as well as conserving the moisture they need and, given this treatment, they will do well.

It is not possible to grow on alkaline soil

members of the ericaceous group, such as rhododendrons. Moreover, lime-induced chlorosis is common among many plants growing on alkaline soil. Calcium has the effect of locking up certain minerals, particularly iron and manganese, causing the leaves to yellow. Heavy dressings of manure, compost and leafmold, all acid substances, are needed to counteract the soil alkalinity and to cure the chlorotic condition.

Most heaths in common with rhododendrons and azaleas and other members of the family *Ericaceae*, sicken and die on limy soils but the winter-blooming *Erica carnea* and its varieties as well as *E. mediterranea* and its hybrids will succeed, particularly if started in peat. Some magnolias, too, in particular *M. kobus*, *M.* × *loebneri*, *M. wilsonii* and *M.* × *highdownensis* will succeed and the rosy-purple *M.* × *lennei* does well in alkaline clay.

Plants for Alkaline Soils

Herbaceous Perennials

Acanthus	Coreopsis	Helianthus	Papaver
Achillea	Dahlia	Helleborus	Primula
Anemone	(moist peat	Hesperis	(primrose and
(Japanese	round tubers)	Incarvillea	polyanthus)
anemones)	Dianthus	Inula	Pulmonaria
Anthemis	Doronicums	Iris (but not	Pulsatilla
Aster	Echinacea	I. kaempferi)	Rudbeckia
Aquilegia	Echinops	Kniphofia	Salvia
Aruncus	Eremurus	Limonium	Scabiosa
Bergenia	Eryngium	Linaria	Sedum
Campanula	Euphorbia	Lysimachia	Solidago
Centaurea	Galega	Macleaya	Stachys
Cephalaria	Geranium species	Nepeta	Thalictrum
Centranthus	Gypsophila	Oenothera	Verbascum
Chrysanthemum	Helenium	Paeonia	Veronica

Bulbs

Agapanthus	Crocus	Gladiolus	Narcissus
Allium	Eranthis	Iris	Nerine
Anemone	Fritillaria	Leucojum	Tulipa
(coronaria)	Galanthus	Lilium	Sternbergia
Colchicum	Galtonia	(some)	Zephyranthes

Shrubs and Trees

Acer	Corylus	Hebe	Pyracantha
(but not the	Cotoneaster	(Veronica)	Quercus
Japanese species)	Crataegus	Hibiscus	Rhus
Aesculus	Cryptomeria	Hippophae	Ribes
Amelanchier	Cupressus	Hypericum	Robinia
Aucuba	Cytisus	Ilex	Rosa species and
Berberis	(but not C.	Indigofera	strong growing
Betula	scoparius)	Jasminum	HTs and
Buddleia	*Daphne mezereum*	Juniperus	Floribundas
Buxus	Deutzia	Kerria	Rosmarinus
Caryopteris	Diervilla	Laburnum	Rubus
Ceanothus	Elaeagnus	Lavandula	Ruscus
Cedrus	*Erica carnea* vars.	Leycesteria	Sambucus
Ceratostigma	*Erica darleyensis*	Ligustrum	Senecio
Cercis	*Erica mediterranea*	Lonicera	Sorbus
Chamaecyparis	vars.	Malus	Spartium
(C. lawsoniana	Escallonia	Osmanthus	Syringa
and vars.)	Euonymus	Paeonia	Taxus
Chaenomeles	Fagus	(Tree paeonies)	Thuja
Chimonanthus	Forsythia	Philadelphus	Thujopsis
Choisya	Fraxinus	Phillyrea	Tilia
Cistus	Fuchsia	Pittosporum	Ulex

1 Candytuft, *Iberis amara*, an annual of 9 - 12 in.

2 *Sedum spectabile*, a Chinese plant flowering in the autumn

3 Hypericum or St. John's Wort, an easy shrub to grow for its flowers and fruit

4 Verbascums flourish in chalky soils. They are apt to appear in unexpected places from self-sown seed

5 *Geranium renardii*, a dwarf kind

5

CHAPTER SEVEN
SHADE GARDENS

Shade plants

Garden shade can vary considerably in density and in its effect on the plants that are growing in it. It ranges from the really deep shade under large trees to the partial shade of a site that faces due east or west and get sunshine for at least half of the day.

Among bulbs and perennials there are plenty of plants which like the shade that are well worth growing. Snowdrops, whether large or small, single or double, all appreciate some shade. So also does the snake's head fritillary, *Fritillaria meleagris*, and scillas of all kinds, together with the winter and summer snowflakes, *Leucojum vernum* and *L. aestivum*.

Wood anemones will make a delightful carpet under trees with their white and pale blue star-shaped flowers and *Cyclamen neapolitanum* and *C. repandum* are equally at home under trees or at the bottom of a shady hedge. Lilies-of-the-valley like woodland shade and act as excellent cover plants once naturalized.

Most lilies prefer a bed with shade around their roots and their heads in the sun. However, they do well in partial shade. In the herbaceous border, the shadier parts can be given up to the lovely species and varieties of hostas and hellebores. The former never display their magnificent foliage to such good effect when they are grown in full sunlight. The plants do well in bright sunshine but foliage is sacrificed to flower production.

Most modern strains of large-flowered polyanthus will adapt to full sunshine, but the flowers last a good deal longer and their color fades less rapidly when the plants are grown in partial shade. Many annuals and biennials will flourish out of the sun, although the plants may be drawn up and the flowers washed out in color. Some, however, do better in partial shade including mallows, foxgloves and honesty. Others, such as love-in-a-mist and nasturtiums, thrive equally well in sun or shade.

Where shady conditions are allied to a really damp soil, you can grow some strikingly exotic plants. Most ferns revel in moist shade and anyone able to meet their re-

quirements should not fail to plant the stately royal fern, *Osmunda regalis*, which reaches a height of 6 ft. or more when established. Other equally interesting plants in this respect are the lysichitums, with their enormous arum-like flowers and handsome paddle-shaped leaves, candelabra primulas such as *P. beesiana* and *P. pulverulenta*, the so-called giant rhubarb, *Gunnera manicata*, and most of the euphorbias.

Among the taller perennials with a preference for moist, shady spots are the goat's beard, *Aruncus sylvester*, with its feathery plumes of meadowsweet flowers, and *Artemisia lactiflora* with 5-ft. spikes of creamy blossom which have a delicate vanilla-like fragrance.

Vinca major and *minor* also make good ground covers. The hardy periwinkles are useful trailing ground cover plants that flower best in the sun, but are quite happy in dry shade beneath a hedge or under trees, in ordinary soil. Once planted leave them undisturbed and allow them to spread, cutting back when necessary in early spring. Propagation is by division or by digging up rooted layers in autumn or early spring. *V. rosea* may be grown in pots

1

2 3

If squirrels visit your garden protect the corms of cyclamen after planting. Spread wire netting over them just under the soil surface

There is a white form of Campanula latifolia which will show up well in shady conditions

of loam and peat; the tips of the shoots should be pinched out to encourage bushiness.

Violas do best in a moist, well-drained soil with light shade.

Large spreading trees such as oak or beech not only rob the soil at their feet of light, but also of both moisture and nourishment. In this kind of situation there are obviously few plants that will flourish successfully apart from certain shrubs such as the butcher's broom, *Ruscus aculeatus*. Its tiny spear-like, evergreen foliage (consisting not of leaves, but of cladodes, or flattened stems) makes a good show in the densest of shade. To enjoy the bright red berries of the butcher's broom, it will be necessary to plant both male and female forms.

An allied but lesser-known plant, *Danaë racemosa* (syn. *Ruscus racemosus*) the Alexandrian laurel, is equally tolerant of shade. Both of these shrubs are of modest dimensions. Neither will exceed much more than 3 ft. in height.

The common and Portuguese cherry laurels will also grow well in dense, dry shade and make some of the finest shrubs for growing in the shadow of oak or beech. The Portuguese laurel, *Prunus lusitanica*, bears almond scented flower spikes and there are few finer evergreen shrubs for covert planting in dense woodland than the common cherry laurel, *Prunus laurocerasus*, with its handsome polished foliage and rapid rate of growth when established.

Another genus of berry-bearing evergreen shrubs, similar in appearance to those already mentioned are the aucubas. The most widely-grown species is the so-called Japanese laurel, *Aucuba japonica*. The variegated forms of this shrub were admired greatly in the last century and they make

1 *Smilacina racemosa*, the False Spikenard, has white flowers in May and red berries in autumn

2 *Campanula latifolia* prefers light shade

3 *Fritillaria meleagris*, Snake's Head

4 *Cyclamen neapolitanum*, a hardy autumn flowering species from the Mediterranean area

5 Cyclamen belong to the same family as the primrose

6 *Cyclamen coum* flowers in late winter and early spring

7 *Cyclamen coum* is easily naturalized at the base of trees

8 *Cyclamen repandum* has scented flowers

excellent shade plants. Like the laurels proper they are excellent as boundary hedges in shady conditions.

Their green and gold variegated leaves bring a feeling of sunshine to the darkest

corners. As well as the type there are some splendid, named varieties, such as "Goldenheart" in which the variegation is much more pronounced than in others. Both of these and the equally attractive green-leaved forms are dioecious (the flowers having one sex only), but they will bear berries freely if plants of both sexes are grown. Where moist humus is more plentiful the choice of suitable shrubs for dense shade becomes much wider. Evergreens such as buxus (box), skimmia, *Mahonia aquifolium* and *Viburnum tinus* (laurustinus) will all flourish. The partridge berries, *Gaultheria procumbens*, grow right to the foot of tree trunks, and species of sarcococca.

Given acid soil conditions *Rhododendron ponticum* will flourish in quite dense shade, although it will also need relatively moist soil. Most rhododendrons, however, thrive best in the light dappled shade at the fringes of woodland or that provided by the lacy foliage of silver birches, sorbus and similar

trees. Camellias and magnolias also grow well in intermittent light and shade, which prevents petal scorch in hot, sunny weather and also protects buds and flowers from severe spring frosts.

Mahonia (ma-ho-ne-a)

At one time the mahonias were included in the same genus *(Berberis)* as the barberries.

1 *Viola gracilis*
2 Ferns of many kinds will naturalize, and meconopses flourish in shade
3 *Epimedium × warleyensis*, a plant for shade, with coppery-red flowers
4 *Magnolia liliflora nigra* will grow satisfactorily in shade
5 The white form of *Viola corruta*, the Horned Violet, from the Pyrenees
6 *Vinca major*, the periwinkle, an evergreen plant useful for banks

variable greens, some glaucous, some with variegated patterns in green, silver and gold. Their flower racemes carry tubular, lily-like blooms mainly in summer, in shades purple-lilac or white. Preferring partial shade, hostas are ideal for mass planting in woodland settings or other shady places. Used in clumbs they discourage weeds from establishing in border edges where they make bold contrast with taller growing plants. As moisture-loving plants they are excellent for planting by streams or on the banks of ponds. When grown in pots or tubs and watered adequately hostas are fine for use in terrace or patio gardening, or in greenhouses and conservatories. Their leaves and flowers last well in water and are used widely in floral arrangements.

Soil preparation should include the addition of well-decayed manure and peat if the soil tends to dry out quickly. Mulch annually in spring with compost or manure. Plant in autumn or spring. Keep moist during dry spells. For pot culture use 2 parts of loam to 1 part of decayed manure and sand mixture. Pot in March or April and over-winter in a cold frame. Hostas are increased by dividing clumps, preferably when new growth starts in spring. Seed in available of some species; this should be sown in spring under glass.

Smilax (smy-laks)
Ancient Greek name of obscure meaning (*Liliaceae*). A genus of some 350 species of hardy, half-hardy and tender twining plants which support themselves by means

The chief distinguishing character of these evergreen shrubs is the pinnate leaf (lacking in *Berberis*) and the fact that the leaves are spiny, while the branches lack spines.

Mahonia (ma-ho-ne-a)
At one time the mahonias were included in the same genus (*Berberis*) as the barberries. The chief distinguishing character of these evergreen shrubs is the pinnate leaf (lacking in *Berberis*) and the fact that the leaves are spiny, while the branches lack spines.

Symphoricapos (sim-for-i-carp-os)
S. albus, snowberry, to 3 ft., spreading by means of runners and thriving in any situation; the large, white berries are conspicuous in autumn and winter; the best form is var. *vigatus* which has also longer shoots, sometimes upward of 6 ft. Few shrubs will thrive in such a variety of soils and situations, from full sun to deep shade. Plant from October to March in suitable weather. Prune in winter by cutting out the oldest wood and any dead wood. Propagation is easily effected by division in winter or spring.

Symphoricarpos albus laevigatus, the snow-berry, and many species and garden varieties of weigela also grow well in full shade. Other excellent shrubs include berberis, *Choisya ternata,* hypericums and *Olearia haastii.*

Hosta (hos-ta)
Commemorating Nicolous Thomas and Joseph Host, Austrian botanists of the late eighteenth and early nineteenth centuries (*Liliaceae*). Plaintain lily. Hardy herbaceous plants, natives of E. Asia, principally Japan, valued for their large decorative leaves in

The florist's smilax is *Asparagus medeoloides,* a tender South African species.

Charming little plants for shade are **maianthemum.** A genus of two or three species only, related to *Smilacina.* They are hardy herbaceous perennials with creeping root-stocks, and racemes of small white flowers. The leaves are rather like those of the lily-of-the-valley (*Convallaria majalis*) and the flowers resemble those of the smilacinas. The maianthemums are useful colonizers of shady places, and once established will need little or no attention.

No special care is needed, although shade from strong sun is desirable, and the plants thrive in thin woodland clearings. Detaching pieces of the creeping rhizomes provides a simple method of propagation.

Another pretty little thing is **smilacina.** With white flowers growing in a loose feathery spike atypical of the lily family, and with parallel-veined leaves.

The soil should be a good loam, moist but not wet. Slightly shaded positions are preferred, in damp woodlands, on banks, in shrub borders or herbaceous borders. Planting is carried out in October or March. Propagation is by division of the roots in the same months as planting.

A plant which seeds itself freely is **tellima.** Said to be an anagran of *Mitella,* from which genus the genus was separated (*Saxifragaceae*). A genus of a single species, *T. grandiflora,* a hardy perennial woodland plant, resembling heuchera. It grows 1½—2 ft. tall, and bears spikes of small, green, bell-shaped flowers, becoming reddish, in May and June. The leaves form a dome of heart-shaped, scalloped foliage, assuming bronze and ruddy tints in autumn.

Plant in autumn or early spring in ordinary garden soil in partial shade, or in a sunny position where the soil does not dry out. Propagation is by division in the spring, or by seed.

A plant useful in flower arrangements as well as a good ground carpeter is **lamium.** Dead nettle. Belonging to the dead nettle family, this herbaceous perennial, from Europe and temperate Asia, is useful as ground cover where other plants, perhaps, would not grow.

L. galeobdolon, 1-1½ ft., yellow, June — July; var. *variegatum,* white variegation on foliage L. maculatum, 8-12 in., white cent-

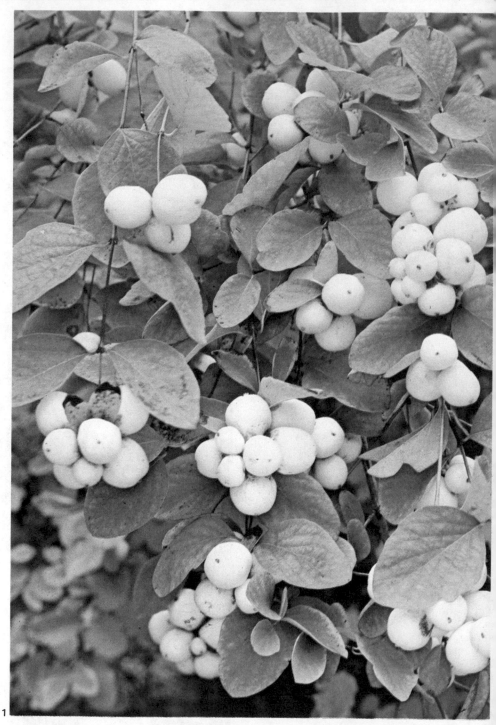

ral stripe on leaves, purple, pink or white flowers, summer, a native plant; var. *aureum,* golden leaves. *L. orvala,* 2 ft., rosy-lilac, summer.

Any garden soil will suit these plants, but *L. maculatum* does best in moist soils,

lamiums can be planted in the autumn or spring and increased by division at any time of the year.

It's nice to have one plant which is so amenable and on which one can rely in a variety of circumstances.

Mahonia leaves dry well. Gather them as soon as they have turned color

If you cut lamium for flower arrangements remove a little of the old stem with each piece. This takes water more easily

1 The white winter berries of *Symphoricarpos albus laevigatus*
2 The long racemes of sweetly scented flowers of *Mahonia japonica*
3 The leaves of *Mahonia bealii* colored well in autumn
4 The blue-black berries of *Mahonia aquifolium* are glaucous
5 Strawberry-like fruits of the1dogwood *Cornus kousa* which
enjoys light shade

CHAPTER EIGHT
SEASIDE GARDENING

Some of the prettiest gardens are at the seaside, but they could never have been made without forethought and sometimes even ingenuity.

There is a very wide range of plants for furnishing the sheltered seaside garden in mild climates. Hybrid escallonias, cistus (in variety), hebes, tree lupins, *Spartium junceum*, *Lavartera olbia*, *Phlomis fruticosa*, hydrangeas, fuchsias, rosemaries and lavenders and all manner of grey-leaved shrubs which should include the cotton lavenders (santolinas), artemisias and helichrysums, all do well by the sea.

Perennial plants may include dianthus where there is lime, dimorphothecas, erigerons, geraniums (cranesbills), echinops, erynigiums, kniphofias, limoniums (sea lavenders), armerias, sedums and mesembryanthemums.

Many shrubs and perennial plants, too tender for frosty inland areas, grow well by the sea when given protection from the worst seawinds, though the range of plants for the colder maritime countries is necessarily more restricted. The almost constant enemies of seaside gardening are wind, salt and sand. Frost, however, is neither so prolonged nor so severe on the coast as it is inland, and seaside gardeners have been able to grow many frost-tender plants in the milder climate of their coastal gardens.

Salt can kill outright. Salt is carried in the spray and when this is caught up by the wind it is often deposited many hundreds of yards inland. Few plants are able to withstand the continual battering of seawind heavily charged with salt, which is scorching to plants.

Sandblast is often too lightly regarded by newcomers to the coast, though its effect can be quite as damaging as that of salt. Seashore gardens suffer badly from its searing effect when the wind picks up the sand

1 See heads on *Fatsia japonica*, an evergreen shrub
2 The hydrangeas do particularly well in exposed seaside localities
3 Lampranthus, members of the *mesembryanthemum* group, flourish by the sea
4 The blooms of *Cistus purpureus*
5 A wall garden where many tender and interesting plants thrive
6 *Abelia grandiflora*
7 Gazanias make a good splash of color during the summer months
8 Hebe "Midsummer Beauty", a good shrub for mild seaside conditions

Coastal wind devastates plants. Only those with protection will escape stunting and deformity

Some of the best shelter trees, such as the maritime and Corsican pines, must be planted when only a foot high. They do not transplant well

from a nearby beach. Small seedlings are killed and mature foliage is bruised and blackened.

Many plants will grow only when given adequate shelter at the outset, and the planting of newly made gardens exposed to the full ravages of gales off the sea is rarely successful without the aid of some artificial windscreen.

Plantings of shelter belts of trees on a large scale benefit from an open fence of a two-bar wooden structure interwoven with foliage. For small gardens there is nothing better than a fence of wooden laths, 1 in. wide with spaces between of similar size, set vertically on a stout wooden framework and posts at either end for driving into the ground. Avoid a solid barricade such as a wall, which causes wind turbulence on the lee side, since the aim is always to filter the wind rather than obstruct it.

Plants which tolerate salt and wind are very largely selected from those grown in Australia and New Zealand. Shrubs that successfully resist salt spray are planted fac-

ing the sea. These are often equipped with toughened leaves such as are found in the genus *Olearia*. *O. haastii* and *O. albida* stand any amount of salty wind. Others have shiny leaf surfaces. *Euonymus japonicus* and *Griselinia littoralis* look bright and glossy within a few yards of the sea. Or the leaves of some may be coated with a gummy secretion as in *Escallonia macrantha*, enabling them to endure a coating of salt. Yet another form of protection is afforded by a multitude of tiny hairs which cover the leaf surfaces of grey-leaved and silver-leaved shrubs. It is a curious fact that most of these are well adapted to withstand the first brunt of a salty blast. Sea buckthorn, *Atriplex halimus*, *Senecio laxifolius* and *S. monroi* are among the best we have for prominent positions in exposed coastal districts. If sandblast is a menace, tamarisk will grow

6

8

with its roots in pure sand and is also useful for adding height to rough banks and walls.

Where there is room to plant, there is no lack of trees for providing shelter. Sycamore, willow and white poplar make useful thickets close to the sea. This enables more worthwhile pines and cypresses to be grown, so that eventually there is a broad streamlined bank of vegetation sloping away from the sea, within the shelter of which many tender plants may thrive.

The best defense against wind is close planting and early thinning. In this way trees are protected when young by being planted close together. Small plants only should be used. These are less at the mercy of the wind and their roots suffer less check by transplanting from the nursery. Since coastal districts are ravaged by salt-laden gales at intervals from October to mid-April, spring planting is best, as this allows 6 months growing weather for plants to establish themselves.

1 *Convolvulus cneorum*
2 *Yucca gloriosa*
3 *Zantedeschia aethiopica*
4 *Cytisus sessifolius*, a shrub for summer show in the seaside garden
5 *Ulex europaeus plenus*
6 *Agapanthus umbellatus*
7 The orange flowers of *Crocosmia crocosmalflora* make a useful display in the late summer and early autumn
8 *Garry aelliptica* has long silky green catkins during the winter months

1

4

2

3

5

6

Sand from the seashore contains salt and should not be used in the garden

The long, ribbon-like seaweed is a valuable manure. It can either be spread fresh on the ground and then dug in, or composted

Shrubs for colder maritime areas

Berberis wilsonae
Buddleia davidii (in variety)
  B. globosa
Caragana arborescens
Caryopteris x clandonensis
Ceanothus x burkwoodii
  C. thyrsiflorus
Cistus corbariensis
  C. ladaniferus
  C. laurifolius
  C. populifolius
Clematis flammula
Colutea arborescens
Coronilla glauca
  C. emerus
Cortaderia argentea
Cotoneasters (in variety)
Crataegus (in variety)
Cytisus battandieri
  C. scoparius hybrids
Elaeagnus ebbingei
  E. pungens aureo-variegata
Escallonia edinensis
  E. x langleyensis
  E. macrantha
Euonymus japonicus
Euphorbia veneta (E. wulfenii)
Garrya elliptica
Genista aethnensis
  G. lydia
  G. hispanica
Griselinia littoralis
Hebe brachysiphon

H. dieffenbachii
H. salicifolia
Hibiscus in variety
Hippophaë rhamnoides
Hydrangeas (in variety)
Hypericum patulum "Hidcote"
  H. androsaemum
Lavandulas (in variety)
Lavatera olbia rosea
Leycesteria formosa
Lonicera ledebourii
Lupinus arboreus
Lycium chinense
Medicago arborea
Olearia albida
  O. haastii
  O. macrodonta
Perovskia atriplicifolia
Phormium tenax
Pittosporum tenuifolium
Potentillas (in variety)
Prunus spinosa
Pyracanthas (in variety)
Ribes alpinum
  R. atrosanguineum
  Romneya x hybrida
Rosa rugosa (and its hybrids)
  R. spinosissima (and its hybrids)
Rosmarinus officinalis
Santolina chamaecyparissus
  S. incana
  S. neapolitana
  S. virens

Senecio laxifolius
  S. monroi
  Spartium junceum
Symphoricarpos orbiculata
  S. microphylla
Tamarix pentandra
Teucrium fruticans
Ulex europaeus plenus
Viburnum tinus
Yucca filamentosa

Some plants for seaside gardens (including tender kinds)

Agapanthus (species and hybrids)
Amaryllis belladonna
Aster pappei
Alstroemeria
Convolvulus mauritanicus
Crambe cordifolia
Crinum (species and hybrids)
Crocosmia masonorum
Dimorphotheca barberiae compacta
  D. ecklonis
Gazanias
Kniphofias
Mesembryanthemums
Montbretia (hybrids)
Myosotidium nobile
Odontospermum maritimum
Othonnopsis cheirifolia
x Venidio-arctotis
Zantesdeschia aethiopica

CHAPTER NINE
FLOWERS FOR FRAGRANCE

All gardeners love scented flowers. My garden is full of fragrant plants, not all of them notable for their flowers alone, for some, such as myrtle, hyssop, rosemary, lavender and the many mints have scented foliage.

It is a perennial complaint of many gardeners that modern cultivars of various plants, particularly roses, lack all or most of the fragrance of the older kinds. Some cultivars are certainly much less fragrant than the "old-fashioned" roses and a few seem to lack detectable fragrance, but, on the whole, a good modern cultivar will number fragrance among its qualities. Much depends, of course, upon the individual sense of smell, coupled with the scent memory which all of us possess to some degree.

In general, it is true that, although the modern roses may be fragrant, the fragrance is lighter than that associated with the "old-fashioned" kinds, which have returned to popularity in recent years, partly because of the rich, heavy fragrance of their blooms. Few gardens are too small to ac-

1 Roses on a trelkis with lavender along the walks
2 The flowers of this *Lilium auratum* hybrid are strongly scented
3 *Jasminum officinale* has heavily scented flowers in late summer
4 An attractive and highly fragrant combination of red roses and white regal lilies
5 *Carpenteria californica*, a free-growing Californian shrub producing its large flowers in July. A sunny position is required
6 A garden in early summer when the fragrant rose "Albertine" is at its best

1

56

Carpenteria deserves to be grown in mild climates but it will not do well in urban areas. It resents atmospheric pollution

Lavender makes a good low-growing hedge

commodate one or two of these; they may not have the perfectly shaped blooms associated with the present-day hybrid tea kinds, but around midsummer, and with some kinds, until late in the season, they will fill the garden with the true rose scent which is difficult to describe precisely, but it is unmistakable when it is found.

Just as distinctive is the true "clove" fragrance of carnations. It is not, alas, found in every cultivar and sometimes those with the most shapely blooms lack fragrance entirely.

It is usually possible to find a corner in which to plant a clump of lilies. But, again, it pays to be careful about the choice of species and cultivars, for not all are fragrant, and some, such as the Turk's cap lily, *Lilium martagon,* have a decidedly unpleasant scent. Even among fragrant types there is a great range of intensity of scent. Among those with the strongest and sweetest

5

6

1 *Choisya ternata* — Mexican Orange — is a shrub that can be grown in the open in mild climates. The fragrant flowers are plentifully produced in April and May
2 *Chimonanthus praecox*, winter-sweet, best grown against a wall in full sun preferably near a path where the fragrance of the flowers can be savored in late winter
3 Nicotiana, the flowering tobacco, is particularly fragrant at dusk
4 *Corylopsis pauciflora* flowers in late winter
5 The late Dutch honeysuckle is fragrant, particularly in the evening
6 *Philadelphus lemoinei* is one of the strongly fragrant mock oranges

fragrance are the regal lily (*Lilium regale*), the Madonna lily (*Lilium candidum*), the golden-rayed lily of Japan (*Lilium auratum*), usually obtainable in its hardier form, *platyphyllum, L. henryi*, and "Crow's Hybrids".

Because they are more permanent than other plants, and need considerably less attention, flowering shrubs are becoming more and more popular. Where space is fairly limited it is worth while choosing some of those with fragrant flowers.

One of the prettiest little early flowering shrubs is corylopsis. Among those flowering in late winter are such fine shrubs as *Hamamelis mollis*, the witch-hazel, with its yellow, cowslip-scented flowers, *Mahonia japomica*, its yellow flowers strongly fragrant, reminiscent of lily-of-the-valley, the sweetly fragrant white *Viburnum fragrans* and *V. tinus*. These are followed in the spring by the *Daphne mezereum*, the lilac-purple flowers of which are thickly clustered along the leafless twigs, the honey-scented, yellow azalea, *Rhododendron luteum*, other viburnums including *V.* x

burkwoodii and *V. carlesii* and the wistarias. Late spring brings the white flowers of *Choisya ternata*, the Mexican orange blossom and the lilacs with their refreshing, unmistakable fragrance. These are soon followed by the mock oranges or philadelphus, their fresh, sweet scent of orange blossom. Among those with the strongest scent are the common *P. coronarius, P. delavayi*, the hybrid *P.* × *lemoinei* and the double-flowered "Virginal".

The sweet jessamine, *Jasminum officinale*, trained against a wall will bring its delicious fragrance through open windows. Lavenders seem to give off their fragrance best on hot summer days, and the spikes of buddleias attract the butterflies.

The climbing honeysuckles come into flower in summer but carry the season on well into the autumn. Again, not all are fragrant but those that are include the late Dutch honeysuckle, *Lonicera periclymenum serotina*, which is usually still producing its reddish-purple flowers in October.

Perennials which have flowers more or less fragrant include the sweet rocket, *Hesperis matronalis, Paeonia*, especially the old

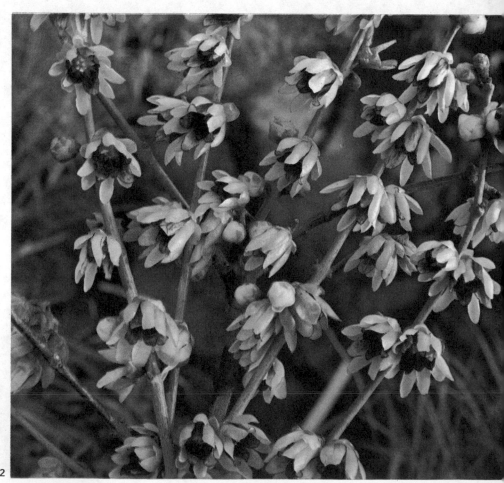

1

2

*The best time to plant chimonanthus is
soon after it has flowered in February.
Prune it at this time, cutting away most
of the shoots that have flowered close to
the base*

*Choisya will grow in any soil, including
those of higher pH. It prefers a sheltered
position and will make a good
and unusual hedge*

cottage garden *paeonias,* varieties of *P. officinalis,* border phloxes, *Astrantia carinthi-
aca,* the perennial wallflower, *Cheiranthus,*
the herbaceous clematis, *C. recta,* the border
pinks and carnations, not all with the
"clove" scent described earlier, and many
kinds of *Viola odorata.*

Of all the easily grown, sweetly scented
annuals, surely the most popular are sweet
peas. Modern varieties yield wonderful

blooms for the minimum of trouble. Other familiar annuals are sweet alyssum flowering tobacco or nicotiana, night scented stock, mignonette, sweet sultan, pot marigold, snapdragon, marvel of Peru and cleome or spider flower.

Nothing scents the spring garden so well as the biennial wallflower, which mingles delightfully with the perfume of daffodils.

Taking them as a group, the bulbous plants include a good many fragrant plants that are well known. The strong but pleasing fragrance of hyacinths is one of the qualities which make them so popular for early forcing in bowls; a few spikes in flower can fill the room.

There are also some fragrant greenhouse bulbs and it is certainly easier to appreciate their fragrance in such close confines than it is in the open air. Freesias, grown in pots, as they usually are, distill an indescribably sweet fragrance. Tuberoses *(Polianthes tuberosa)* are not grown as often as they were years ago, but the tubers are obtainable and are well worth growing for the sake of the wonderful scent of the flowers in autumn and winter. Here, perhaps, is the place to bring in the lily-of-the-valley *(Convallaria majalis)* because it is so easily forced in boxes, or grown in pots, either for greenhouse use or for bringing into the living room when the plants are in flower. They can be grown out of doors, particularly in a shady moist spot, just as various other hardy fragrant plants such as lilacs, narcissus and lilies of various kinds may either be grown outside or in pots in the greenhouse, usually flowering a little earlier, even when very little heat is available. Where more heat is available in winter it is possible to grow such fragrant flowers as stephanotis, acacias (usually miscalled mimosa), carnations, bouvardias, the little annual *Exacum affine*, gardenias, *Hoya carnosa*, *Jasminum polyanthum* and other tender jasmines, the jasmine-scented *Trachelospermum jasminioides*, the lily-scented *Datura arborea* as well as many others.

1 Sweet pea "Bijou", a low-growing type which carries a good crop of flowers
2 "Hidcote", a deep, purple-blue form of *Lavandula spica*, useful for low hedges

Although some seedsmen apply the term "hardy annual" to many of the stocks, it is not advisable to give hardy annual treatment to any but the night flowering Matthiola bicornis

Rosa gallica is said to have been brought from Damascus by the Crusaders and hence known as the Red Damask

3 The deep pink flowers of *Rosa gallica* "Surpass Tout" are fully double
4 *Rosa gallica* "Cardinal Richelieu" has maroon flowers
5 The Tree lupin, a quick-growing shrubby plant, is delicately perfumed
6 The various types of stock have been derived from *Matthiola incana*.
They can be obtained in various shades of pink and purple, and in white.

CHAPTER TEN
PATIO PLANTS

Patio gardens

The patio, as a feature of our gardens, has been popular for many years. The word patio, in fact, is something of a misnomer; its original Spanish meaning referred to an *inner* court or enclosed space open to the sky, a feature commonly encountered in Spanish and South American houses.

Today, the description is applied to almost any kind of outdoor paved space adjacent to the house.

It can be a delightful feature allied to both house and garden and an ideal way both of displaying and caring for beautiful plants.

With many new houses, the patio becomes an integral part of the design, having been planned that way by the architect. This is a particularly satisfactory procedure, since it can be correctly located to take full advantage of sun and shelter. At the planning stage, too, it is possible to arrange for an outdoor hearth with the chimney connecting to those of the indoor fireplaces.

Plants on the patio should be mainly climbing and wall shrubs and any other plants suitable for growing in tubs, urns and other containers. Decorative tubs and jardinières are obtainable in terracotta and natural or artificial stone. Antique pots and figures are costly and increasingly hard to come by, but there are plenty of effective substitutes in artificial stone and other similar materials. Lead urns and cisterns, too, now sell for very high prices. It is possible, however, to obtain reproductions of old ones that are authentic in every detail, down to the grey-green patina that lead acquires with age and exposure to weather. Even these are not exactly cheap, but their cost is only a fraction of that of the genuine article.

Several shapes and sizes are available from terrace-type pots which are large enough to hold small shrubs or a mass of bedding plants to bulb bowls and troughs. They are ideal containers for the woman gardener as they are light and pleasant to handle. They must be used with care, however, as they are fairly fragile when filled. For example, it is not wide to pull a large trough, when filled, by its rim, as this can break off easily. A long trough must be supported underneath with a piece of timber if it has to be moved when filled. Usually, however, containers should be placed in their correct positions first and then filled and planted.

Some window-box or plant trough designs are manufactured from strong plastic materials which result in lightweight, rot-proof articles. They also have particular ap-

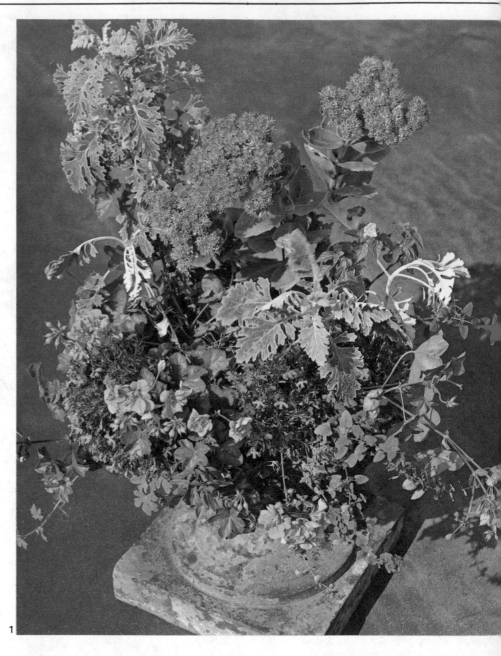

1

peal to the gardener as they are attractively decorated by relief designs. Suitable plastic and fiberglass shallow plant troughs can be obtained for indoor use. These are ideal for placing pot plants in, especially on the window ledge. A few small pebbles in the bottom plus a regular supply of small amounts of water will provide the ideal moist atmosphere for growing many plants. There are several fiberglass plant tubs on the market. These are made from special high-quality fiberglass in various colors, such as red, yel-

low and green. The material used in thei construction is light, so the containers ar easy to handle. As their coloring is perma nent, there is no need to paint them an they will not rot or warp.

Fiberglass is also used for troughs, win dow boxes, urns and other types of plan container.

Plants grown on the walls adjacent to th patio are best grown in beds. This, how ever, may not always be practicabl because of damp courses, drains or othe

A patio can provide an effective link between the formality of the house and the informality of the garden

The materials used for the construction of a patio should be in harmony with those used for the house

3

4

1 Flowering and foliage plants
grown in urns, ornamental vases,
plant boxes of many kinds, tubs
and large pots, will all help to
furnish the balcony garden
2 Rectangular tiles make a clean
path to the house
3 *Fuchsia fulgens,* a greenhouse
species, has long, coral-scarlet
flowers
4 Fuchsia is effective
when planted in a large
container. The pale yellow-green
foliage, with red veins and stems,
is a good background for the
coral-magenta flowers
5 Round units are used to pave
this patio. Plants in pots and in
beds surrounded by a low wall
provide color
6 Fuchsia, "Beauty of Bath",
a free-flowering hardy
cultivar

6

constructional hazards. But many climbers will do quite well in tubs or boxes. Although their rate of growth may be slowed down considerably, this is not necessarily a disadvantage, as it enables a greater variety of plant to be grown.

Actual plants used will depend largely on the tastes of the gardener. The following suggestions are based on experience of what will grow well on a patio and give the pleasure of longlasting color. Marigolds (tagetes), Virginian stocks (*Malcolmia maritima*), campanulas, nasturtiums (*Tropaeolum majus*), annual or China asters (callistephus), lobelias, nemesia, impatiens, wallflowers (cheiranthus), petunias, forget-me-nots (myosotis), pansies, arabis, periwinkle (vinca), pelargoniums, *Saxlfraga saramentosa,* stonecrops (sedums) and houseleeks (sempervivums), crocuses, dwarf tulips, daffodils and hyacinths, antennaria, zinnias, mesembryanthemums, dwarf antirrhinums and many more. All are comparatively low growing.

In winter, patio gradens just cannot be a blaze of color, but the troughs and pots need not be empty. Winter-flowering heathers (*Erica carnea* and others), variegated ivies (hederas), aucuba, dwarf conifers, skimmia, *Osmanthus delavayi, Mahonia aquifolium, Senecio laxifolius,* and a small camellia or two are all worth growing where there is space.

There are certain top favorites as one would expect and fuchsias are one of these. Window boxes are decorative when filled with such cultivars as "Benitchea", "Evening Sky", "Santa Lucia", "Sicna Blue", "Tinker Bell", because they cascade slightly over the sides of the box.

Because I love scented plants I grow heliotrope, which is easily raised from seed. By taking cuttings in autumn or spring a

1 Round slabs, used in conjunction with infilling pieces, are used to pave this patio garden
2 A formal patio where a dripping fountain provides a sense of coolness
3 Well-stocked plant tubs on a brick-paved terrace
4 A "Chilstone" reproduction of a Regency basket plant container
5 Heliotrope, "Cherry Pie", a summer flowering plant grown for its perfume
6 Concrete slabs are used in contrasting colors to provide a formal pattern for this patio

1

2

Plant containers made from polystyrene rapidly assimilate warmth. This keeps the soil in them much warmer than in clay or stone pots

Old barrels sawed in half make excellent tubs. Make drainage holes in the base

supply of small plants for pot work or for bedding out of doors can be maintained, autumn rooted cuttings usually making the better plants. Pinch out the tops when about 5 in. of growth has been made to produce bushy plants. Water frequently and fertilize before flowering. Standard heliotropes are obtained by stopping at the desired height and side shoots stopped subsequently to form a head.

So, for complete success you need the right plants and the right soil. More about both these subjects in the next section.

5

3

4

6

CHAPTER ELEVEN
WINDOW BOXES

1

2

3

Fixing A window box on a high sill that
not securely fixed can be dangerous, so us
long hasps and staple fittings to secure th
box to the window frame. It is better to pre
pare the box actually located on the windo
ledge, as this saves carrying a box full of so
to the ledge and placing it in what is ofte
an awkward position. Lay broken crocks o
the bottom of the box at about ½ in. deep t
prevent soil being washed out of the drain
age holes and at the same time giv
adequate drainage. On top of this a fibrou
material such as peat should be laid. Th
soil mix can be made with 3 parts of loam (c
good garden soil), 1 part of peat or leafmol
and 1 part of sharp sand. To each bushe
add 2 or 3 handfuls of bonemeal. The so
should be changed every 2 or 3 years, or th
top 2 or 3 inches should be replaced wit
fresh soil or compost.

Planting Pelargoniums or fuchsias, in as
sociation with alyssum or lobelia, togethe
with foliage plants, such as coleus, or th
grey-leaved *Senecio cineraria,* will provide
summer display requiring little mainte
nance. Hardy and half-hardy plants, in
cluding stocks, zinnias and verbenas, a
give a longlasting display if the dead flow
ers are picked off regularly. Tobacco plant
French and African marigolds also make
good effect.

Begonias (both tuberous and fibrous
rooted species), ferns, fuchsias, creepin
Jenny (*Lysimachia nummularia*) wit
periwinkles, *Tradescantia fluminensis,* an
the smaller ornamental ivies, are suitabl
for a north-facing aspect. Where there
partial shade only (northeast and northwe
aspects), begonias, pelargoniums, lobeli
alyssum and phacelias all do well. Climbin
plants should be planted at the walls o
either side of the window with suitabl
supports.

Climbing nasturtiums will cling to string
or wires; *Ipomoea* ''Heavenly Blue'' (morr
ing glory) likes a sheltered, sunny positior

More permanent climbers are the com
pact ivies, such as *Hedera helix aureovariega*
or the smaller leaved ''Buttercup''. Vine
also the Virginian creeper, *Parthenocissu*
quinquefolia, or the smaller leaved, mor
compact *P. henryana,* are all suitable.

Bulbs One of the best times of year fo
a window box is early in the year whe
daffodils, tulips, hyacinths, scillas
chionodoxas and other bulbs are flowering

Hardwood window boxes can be oiled or varnished. Softwoods should be treated with preservatives (never creosote) and can be painted

Timber for window boxes should be at least ½ in. thick and the inside depth should be 7-10 in.

4

1 A well planted window box
2 Pelargoniums make fine
window box decoration
3 A window box planted for
summer effect with colored
foliage plants requires a minimum
of attention
4 Because of their exposed
situations some balconies will
need protection from wind. It is
often possible to glass in one end
of the balcony to provide shelter
5 Balcony gardens can be made
colorful in summer by using
annual plants

5

CHAPTER TWELVE
HANGING BASKETS

Hanging baskets

I wonder who first thought of making a hanging basket? What decorative little gardens these are, and yet we often see those that haven't quite come off. It is apparent that many people do not realize that a beautiful hanging basket does not just happen. Like the other types of gardens already discussed (window boxes and patio containers) none must be neglected. It is essential to use good soil of a proper texture and rich in humus and nutrients. I have also noticed that the loveliest hanging baskets are always those which are in shade during some part of the day, the best being those shaded from the midday sun.

The use of hanging baskets is a simple but very attractive way of decorating a porch or terrace during the summer. Baskets may also be hung from the rafters of a greenhouse, for decoration during most of the year. They can be bought in varying sizes, from 10-18 in. in diameter and 6-9 in. deep.

Baskets are made of stout galvanized wire in an open mesh or a wave design or of green, plastic-coated, rustproof wire, in the same patterns. Plastic baskets are also available in green, red, white, yellow and blue, and can be purchased with a special drainage device. In greenhouses, square wooden containers made of slats are often used, particularly for orchids of trailing habit, such as *Stanhopea*.

For safety's sake baskets should be hung from strong hooks, well above eye level where they cannot obscure the light or a view or be knocked about as people pass under them.

Planting the basket Wedge the basket in the top of a large bucket, bowl or box to hold it firm while the planting is done. Line it with damp sphagnum moss; about half a gallon of this will be required to make a good lining. Alternatively, thick polyethylene can be used to line the basket, when holes will need to be punched in the base for drainage, although it is possible to purchase perforated polyethylene which is quite suitable. Polyethylene does not look as decorative as sphagnum moss but holds the moisture better and if the basket cannot be given daily attention it is probably better to use this material, although a thin layer of peat packed within the sphagnum moss lining will help considerably with water retention.

If sphagnum moss is not available, hay, packed tightly round the interior of the basket, is an adequate substitute.

Some gardeners like to put a small plastic saucer in the base to catch and retain some of the water, and to reduce drip to some extent.

A reasonably rich compost is best because the small amount that can be accommodated has to provide sustenance for a fairly extensive root system. Do not attempt to get too many plants into one basket. A 12-in. diameter basket will hold three plants from 5 in. pots, plus several smaller or trailing plants between them and around the edge.

Choose plants that are just coming into flower, turn them out of their pots and fill the well of the basket with compost, firming it with the fingers. Place the larger plants in position, angling them slightly toward the edge. At this stage small plants such as lobelia and alyssum can be tucked between the mesh of the basket so that eventually the flowers will clothe the sides. Continue to pack in the soil round the root balls and make it firm, leaving a slight depression or well on the surface of the soil — another trick to conserve moisture and to prevent water from overflowing when the basket is watered. The surface should be about 2 in. below the rim of the basket. Seeds of nas-

turtiums can be pushed into strategic positions at this stage. Immerse the basket in water, then allow it to drain before hanging it up.

In an unheated greenhouse far more elaborate baskets can be planted during early May. The baskets are lined and filled with compost and carefully inverted on the staging, when young plants of coleus, chlorophytum or tolmiea can be pushed

2

through the structure of the basket and firmed with a dibber. Leave the basket in this position for 2 or 3 weeks before turning it right way up and planting up the rest of in the usual way. The ideal way of holding basket partially prepared in this way while the remaining planting is done is to construct a triangle of laths which can be laid over a bin to wedge the basket without damaging the plants already there. It will be necessary to scoop out some of the compost before planting up the top. Water very thoroughly, while the basket is still in the planting position.

Maintenance Avoid position in full sun or deep shade; the former dries out the arrangement too quickly and the latter discourages showy flowering, although such positions are suitable for baskets planted with ferns for foliage effect. Water 3 or times a week, daily or even twice daily during very hot weather, adding a flower fertilizer to the water at the recommended rate once a week, after flowering has started. Water from above, allowing the basket to drain if possible to avoid leaching out the plant food; otherwise immerse it for a few

1

To reach a hanging basket tie the hose to a cane

Plastic hanging baskets with a built-in drip tray are now available. These simplify watering and feeding

minutes in a tub of water and allow surplus to drain away before hanging it up again.

Watering a hanging basket from above can be difficult unless one stands on steps. It can, of course, be lifted off its hook but a large basket full of earth and plants can be quite heavy and awkward. One way of dealing with this problem is to fix a small pulley in place of the hook. Strong cord, or preferably strong pliable wire or chain, is fixed to the suspension ring of the basket and passed over the pulley. The other end is attached to a hook fixed on the nearest wall. The basket may then be lowered for watering and easily raised again.

Wash the leaves occasionally and snip off dead flower heads to keep a well-groomed appearance.

Suggested plants The following is a list of plants suitable for basket cultivation. Those marked (G) are more suitable for *Flowering plants for summer display*: Achimenes; Ageratum; Begonia "Gloire de Lorraine" and pendulous kinds such as "Mrs. Bilkey," "Fleur de Chrysantheme", "Golden Shower", "Lena", "Meteor"; *Begonia semperflorens* for mild localities; Calceolaria; *Campanula isophylla* and *C. isophylla alba*; *Chrysanthemum frutescens* (marguerite); *Columnea banksii* (G); Fuchsia, drooping varieties such as "Cascade", "Golden Marinka", "La Bianco", "Marinka", "Thunderbird"; Heliotrope; *Hoya bella* (G); *Lantana camara* for mild localities; *Lobelia pendula* and *L. tenuior*; *Lobularia maritima* (sweet Alison); Pelargonium, upright zonal kinds for top of basket, ivy-leaved varieties for draping the sides, such as "Abel Carriere", "Edward VII", "Galilee", "L'Elegance", "Madame Crousse", "Madame Morrier"; Petunia, especially "Balcony Blended" strain; Tropaeolum (nasturtiums), especially climbers or trailers; Verbena, dwarf and trailing *Perennials*: Aubrieta; *Campanula portenschlagiana*; *Cerastium tomentosum*; *Cymbalaria muralis*; *Glechoma hederaefolia*; *Lysimachia nummularia*; *Vinca minor*. *Foliage plants*: *Adiantum cuneatum* (G); *Adiantum gracillimum* (G); *Asparagus sprengeri* (G); Chlorophytum (G); Coleus (G); *Davallia canariensis* (G), Hedera (ivy) in variety; *Nephrolepis exalta* (G), *Nephrolepis fosteri* (G), *Saxifraga sarmentosa*; Smilax (G); *Tolmiea menzisii* (G); *Tradescantia fluminensis* (G); Zebrina in variety (G).

Bulbs: (for late winter and spring display) Crocus, *Narcissus* (daffodil), *Galanthus* (snowdrop), Tulip (double).

1 A small hanging basket, planted with fuchsias and pelargoniums
2 Ivy-leaved pelargoniums are ideal for providing a showy basket
3 A floriferous begonia in a basket
4 Browallia, a greenhouse flowering annual, makes a decorative trailing plant for a hanging basket

3

CHAPTER THIRTEEN

MINIATURE GARDENS

Miniature gardens

The prettiest gardens are not always the biggest, neither are the keenest gardeners found only in large gardens.

Where space is really limited there is only one answer. Design and planting must be scaled down to fit the area available. But gardening on this reduced scale can be just as rewarding. In these pygmy plots, the opportunity for healthy exercise may be lacking, but to many gardeners, especially the elderly and those who prefer to "putter", this may not necessarily be a great disadvantage.

Miniature gardens can take a number of forms. In the very small plot, you can share the pleasures of those who work on a broader canvas by restricting your planting, not only to single specimens of your favorite plants, but also by growing those that are compact in habit with a slow rate of increase.

The miniature garden proper, however, will not be able to rely on such measures. For its impact, it will have to depend mainly on dwarf plants, some of which may be miniature replicas of their taller counterparts while others will display their own individual characteristics.

Fortunately there are many small forms of familiar and lovely flowering plants. They include shrubs of many kinds including lavender, azaleas, rhododendrons and ericas, and little violas, anchusa, hardy geraniums, irises and many bulbs.

Miniature rose gardens Miniature roses have become generally popular in recent years. One of their main attractions lies in the opportunity that they afford of enjoying the beauty of roses where space would not permit the planting of a rose garden of the orthodox kind.

Sometimes known as fairy roses, many of these delightful dwarfs bear a strong resemblance to popular hybrid tea roses and floribundas. Others have equally delightful individual characteristics.

Little interest was shown by gardeners in these pygmy roses until after World War II. These, apart from their compact habit, include permanence and a very long flowering season.

Many of the miniature roses stem from the dainty *Rosa rouletti,* a tiny rose that was discovered in a Swiss cottage garden by a Dr. Roulet and named in his honor. From this charming miniature have evolved, directly or indirectly, many of the loveliest miniatures available today, including "Tom Thumb", "Pixies" and "Midget".

Miniature roses are extremely hardy. They come into flower early and continue to produce their flowers throughout the summer and autumn. They are best planted from pots as they do not like root disturbance. This makes it possible to plant them at almost any time of year although March and April are the best months for this operation. Those planted in summer should be given plenty of water during dry spells in their first season.

The many named forms now available can be used to create a complete rose garden in miniature or can be incorporated as a separate feature of a larger garden. They are also useful for permanent dwarf bedding schemes.

All the features of a full-sized rose garden can be incorporated, scaled down, of course, to suitable dimensions. Pygmy pergolas, trellises and small rustic screens can

1

2

Raised beds in a tiny garden bring plants nearer eye level

Many alpine or rock garden plants are ideal for little gardens. Many grow flat on the ground and do not need rocks

out. They can be used, as well, for another kind of miniature garden, the window box, provided that the latter is at least 9 in. deep.

Among those most widely grown are "Baby Gold Star" (golden yellow), "Bit O' Sunshine" (gold), "Humoreske" (deep pink), "Little Buckaroo" (scarlet with white center), "Sparkle" (single scarlet) and the midget rose that started it all, *Rosa rouletti*.

"Baby Masquerade", a newer introduction, is a perfect replica, in miniature, of the favorite floribunda of the same name, with clusters of flowers that produce the typical kaleidoscope of color of the latter.

This rose, together with "Cinderella" (pale pink edged white), "Coralin" (coral-pink) and "Maid Marion" is obtainable in standard form. There are climbing forms of the bright pink "Perla Rosa", the yellow and orange "Little Showoff", which is practically perpetual-flowering and "Baby Crimson", which is also known as "Perla d'Alcanada", "Pink Cameo", too, makes an attractive climber. None of these climbing miniatures exceeds 4−5 ft. in height.

A good way of getting horticultural quarts into pint pots is to garden in sinks and troughs. Several of these plant contain-

be used to support climbing varieties, while miniature standards will emphasize focal points and act as central features of miniature bedding schemes.

Miniature roses need only a minimum of attention where pruning is concerned. This operation is best carried out with a sharp pair of small scissors. It consists mainly of removing weak growths and cutting back dead or diseased shoots to healthy wood. It is carried out in spring.

These small roses thrive best in similar types of soil to those in which the hybrid tea roses and floribundas do well. They like a fairly heavy, slightly acid loam, rich in humus. Lack of humus can be remedied by forking in well-rotted animal manure or garden compost, a few weeks before planting. If neither of these is available, peat or leafmold, mixed with bonemeal makes a satisfactory substitute.

These dwarf roses will also flourish and look well in the old stone troughs already mentioned; the sinks are too shallow and there would be a danger of the roots drying

1 Miniature gardens made up of saxifrages, sedums, campanulas, arenarias, lewisias and miniature conifers
2 Androsaces, houseleeks, lewisias, dwarf conifers and other alpine plants make an interesting small garden
3 A permanent rock garden in miniature can be established in stone trough or sink
4 Although bonsai trees such as this have the appearance of great age, it is possible, by careful training, to produce specimens in a few years. Many trees may be trained in this way, both deciduous and evergreen

ers, each with its separate planting scheme, can be accommodated in a minimum of space. Many a backyard or balcony could benefit from the inclusion of a feature of this kind.

Unfortunately, genuine stone troughs and sinks are fast becoming collectors, items and, in consequence, increasingly difficult and expensive to buy. The stone sinks of Victorian kitchens and sculleries have long ago been replaced by vitreous enamel and stainless steel while the larger troughs, formerly used for watering cattle and horses, have given place to galvanized iron tanks.

The occasional specimen still turns up at country sales and in junkyards, but dealers are aware of their value and prices have risen astronomically. As an alternative, concrete or old glazed sinks can be adapted for the purpose. But neither of these will have the charm of the genuine article which, if it has been out-of-doors for any length of time, will be weathered and decorated with mosses and lichens.

Particular attention must be paid to drainage before planting any of these containers. A piece of perforated zinc should cover the existing drainage hole and the base of the trough or sink should be covered with broken crocks or stone chips to a depth of 2−3 in. On top of this goes a layer of peat moss or sod, the latter grass side down.

The planting mixture should consist of 2 parts of loam to 1 part of peat and 1 part of sharp sand, with a dusting of lime or the addition of mortar rubble. The lime content must be omitted where ericaceous plants, such as dwarf rhododendrons, are to be planted.

Among the many plants that can be grown successfully in a sink or trough garden are the hardier small saxifrages, sempervivums (houseleeks), thrift and other alpine plants of tough constitution. In a shady situation, mossy saxifrages, hardy cyclamen and miniature ferns will flourish.

For more permanent effects, use can be made of some of the dwarf shrubs and conifers mentioned below.

One way of entering a new world of gardening, is to train the eye to new visions and the fingers to new skills by cultivating bonsai.

Bonsai

The Japanese word *bonsai* literally means "planted in a shallow vessel", but it is now usually restricted to trees or shrubs artificially dwarfed.

The Japanese have a great number of

"styles" for bonsai, including some which combine several specimens, and books on the subject will also illustrate some ingenious "short cuts", such as laying a sapling

down horizontally to make it produce vertical shoots which are then dwarfed.

Remember that a bonsai specimen is no just a stunted tree: it is a work of ar achieved after years of almost daily attention.

The ideal bonsai tree is one which ha been naturally dwarfed in the wild state perhaps growing in a rock cranny or in very exposed position. The Japanese priz such trees very highly, all the more as infi nite care and patience is needed to extrac them, which might be done over severa months. The Japanese also air-layer rugge or unusually shaped portions of tre branches.

The normal method of producing a bon sai tree, however, is to start with seed

1 Deficits of rainfall can be made up by watering, and "artificial rain" provides a gentle supple of water over a long period
2 Dwarf conifers of many kinds are ideal for miniature gardens
3 A splendid collection of trough gardens, each one planted up in an individual way with succulents and miniature conifers
4 One of the troughs, which contains a selection of houseleeks

Watering bonsai is vital. In hot, dry weather plunge the tree and its container under water until bubbles cease to rise from the soil surface. This will ensure that the soil is evenly moist

A fine spray of clean water over the foliage will do much to refresh the tiny trees on a summer day

seedlings or rooted cuttings. Seedling trees can be found in the countryside, and those which are naturally stunted or unusually shaped are good starting points. Almost any kind of tree or shrub can be used, though conifers are probably the easiest to train. (Naturally dwarf forms of conifers are not suitable for bonsai as they seldom respond to training.)

The points to aim for in a bonsai tree are that it should be aesthetically pleasing and well proportioned — mere distortion is not the aim. It should have a stout trunk, and the root growth and top growth must be in balance.

Growing from seed allows complete control over the whole process. Seed should be fresh and is sown in shallow pans or boxes of sandy loam, placed in a cold frame or in a cool place outside, shaded from sun. Germination sometimes takes a long time, but once the seedlings appear and are an inch or two high they should be transferred to individual small containers. Small flowerpots or waxed paper containers (e.g. ice cream tubs punctured with drainage holes) can be used, and a popular method is to plant in a

dried half-orange or grapefruit skin. It is important to prevent the containers from drying out.

During the first year root pruning will be needed once, or possibly twice. If the plant is in an orange skin or a carton, the roots will grow through and should be cut off as they appear. Plants in pots must be taken out and any long thick roots cut out, the fibrous roots being trimmed lightly. The purpose of root pruning at any stage is not to weaken the plant but to encourage the formation of a mass of active roots in a small space.

Any vigorously growing shoots that appear should be pinched out with finger and thumb, though too many leaves must not be removed at once.

In the second season the young tree grows rapidly and needs constant attention; this season really determines the success of the final product. The roots need cutting back in spring and in mid-summer, preceding this by the picking away of some of the soil with a pointed stick. After root trimming, repot very firmly in the same container, adding fresh soil.

In the third year the tree can be placed in its permanent container, which should be glazed and relatively shallow. From this time on a spring root trim is sufficient, but unwanted shoots must be continually pinched out as they appear. Keep the ultimate desired shape of the bonsai firmly in mind, achieving this not only by pinching, but if necessary, by wiring the branches with very soft wire spiraled around them, or by weighting or tying down the branches. Crowded or crossing branches should be avoided.

The annual trim and repotting is an opportunity to lift the tree out of the soil a little each time, exposing the base of the trunk and the upper roots. Shade from direct sun is desirable, but the trees need plenty of light and air, and, of course, adequate water. A little weak liquid fertilizer may be given every 2 or 3 weeks in the growing period, especially in the early years.

Suitable soil mixtures are as follows: Deciduous trees: 6 parts of loam, 2 parts of rotted leafmold, or peat, 1 part of course sand. Conifers: 6 parts of loam, 1 part of leafmold or peat, 3 parts of coarse sand.

3

4

CHAPTER FOURTEEN
WINDOW SILL PLANTS (INDOORS)

1

2

There is a great difference between house and window sill plants. In the first group are those which will grow in many places in the home. The others need a high light intensity, though not necessarily strong and direct sunlight. They are in fact those plants which are usually grown or raised in a greenhouse but which will tolerate the dryer conditions of a living room.

Cyclamen

Many people begin this kind of gardening by being given a plant, a cyclamen for instance. Water moderately and fertilize throughout the flowering period which can be from November to March. Remove old blossoms and leaves by tugging them out from the base of the stem. After flowering, gradually dry off, resting the tubers out of doors in a dry frame during the summer months.

In August soak the pot and tuber that have previously been dried off all summer and once the tiny leaves begin to sprout, repot in a fresh compost of 2 parts of loam to 1 part of leafmold and sand. The tuber should be potted so that the level of the soil surrounds its circumference, no deeper. Keep close for a few days until growth starts again. Syringe daily, keep the plants shaded and maintain a moist atmosphere and temperature of 55-60°F.

Propagation is from seed sown in very fine soil between mid-August and mid-November in a temperature of 50-60°F. Prick off the seedlings and then pot them into small pots. Subsequently pot them on, with the necks of the tubers well above soil level.

Coleus Every year raise some coleus from seed in pans on a warm window sill.

Use a loose fertile potting mixture in 5-6 in. pots. Keep adequately warm and moist. Summer temperatures, 60-65°F, winter, 55°F, minimum, 45°F. Water well during the warm season, less so during the cooler months. Fertilization is beneficial throughout summer. Propagation is by seed sown

1 Modern strains of cyclamen produce large elegant blooms on strong stems
2 This group shows the sturdy growth and the wide variety in color of cyclamens
3 There are many forms of *Coleus blumei*, all grown for their brilliantly colored leaves
4 The double-flowered begonias 4 and 5 are examples of the large-flowered hybrids. "Flamingo" 6 is one of a number of *Begonia semperflorens* types often used for summer bedding. The Rex Begonias 7 are grown for their colorful leaves

3

Tuberous begonias must be gradually dried out after they have flowered. Leave them in the pot, store in a frost-proof shed or knock them out and store in clean, dry sand

Coleus shoots will root in water. They can then be potted to make new plants

in February, March and April, barely covered in a temperature of 70°F, or by cuttings of young shoots taken at almost any time. Top young plants by pinching out the growing point to induce bushiness.

Begonia These are deservedly popular plants, whether the foliage or the flowering kinds.

The genus begonia is usually divided into two groups; those species with fibrous roots and those with tubers. Other classifications give special treatment to the winter-flowering forms, and to those grown exclusively for the interest of their leaves. A notable feature of begonias is their oblique, lopsided or uneven sided leaves.

The fibrous-rooted begonias are usually obtained from seed, which should be sown in January in a temperature of 60°F. It is also possible to make cuttings taken from the base of the plant. The sub-shrubby peren-

6

4

5

7

nial forms will come easily from normal cuttings, or all begonias may be raised by leaf cuttings.

Most begonias need a winter temperature of about 60°F. The ornamental Rex type must not be exposed to full sunlight, and many of the other classes will be happy with much less light than suits other greenhouse plants.

The tuberous begonias are usually started into growth by placing them in shallow boxes of peat or leafmold in February or March, hollow side uppermost, in a temperature of 60-70°F. After roots have formed, the tubers are potted up in small pots and later moved into larger ones.

Do not start to fertilize these tuberous plants till they have formed roots, or they will decay, but after they are rooted a bi-

weekly dose of liquid fertilizer is helpful. The tuberous begonias may also be raised from seed, and if this is sown in February plants may flower from July to October.

Epiphyllums Tremendous delight can be had from a few epiphyllums or leaf-flowering cacti. They give wonderful flowers without much trouble.

These plants are easily grown and will thrive in almost any type of soil. Encourage new growth each year as this will flower more freely. Repot when plants become potbound, water them freely from April to September. Keep them in the greenhouse in winter and spring, but place them out

By crossing epiphyllum 1 "London Magic" with 3 "London Glory" the unpredictability of seedlings from hybrid parents is demonstrated. Most of the progeny are like

2 "London Sweetheart" and show blends of salmon and carmine pink. Among the seedlings was 4 "London Sunshine" which was quite unexpected since no yellow could be seen in either parent, and yellow is rare in epiphyllums. Moreover, the parents are scentless but half the seedlings, including "London Sweetheart" and "London Sunshine", are scented
5 *Rhipsalidopsis rosea* "Electra" has pendent pink flowers
6 *Zygocactus truncatus*, the Christmas cactus, produces cerise-red flowers in winter
7, 8, 9 Hybrid hippeastrums
10 Hippeastrum "Picotee" a pale cream with a green throat

Zygocactus can be grafted onto a tall understock to make an umbrella-shaped specimen

Epiphyllum cuttings are easily obtained from young shoots. Even a section will make roots if the cut part is first allowed to dry. Root them in sharp sand

5

7

8

9

6

10

doors for summer. These plants do not like strong sunshine.

Until recently only a comparatively limited range of color was available, but these plants have responded to plant breeding in a most exciting way. Other colors from the species are now available from specialist growers. The pictures tell their story.

These plants grow quite large, but there are smaller species, rhipsalis and the popular zygocactus or Christmas cactus. The need similar care.

For zygocactus...

Repot every 2 years or when the plant becomes too large for its pot, repotting when flowering has ceased. In winter maintain a minimum temperature of 50°F, increasing this to 60°F as buds form. Water when the soil has almost dried out, throughout the winter. In May or June plants may be placed out of doors in semi-shade. Give them a weak liquid fertilizer after flowering. When plants are in bud do not move them and at this time, in particular, protect them from drafts. The causes of bud drop are too wet or too dry a soil or a changeable atmosphere. Propagation is by cuttings which are best taken in early summer and rooted in sharp sand, spraying them occasionally. Or plants may be grafted on to *Pereskie* stock.

Hippeastrum *(hip-pe-as-trum)*

Growing a plant until it produces a wonderful flower brings a great sense of achievement. Hippeastrums are tremendously rewarding in this respect.

A genus of S. American bulbous plants often referred to as *Amaryllis,* to which they are closely related. The large, showy, trumpet flowers of the hybrids, ranging in color from the richest velvety crimson to the more delicate shades of pink and white, also bicolored, rank them among the most prized of winter and spring flowering pot plants for the greenhouse. Most of the hippeastrums offered in trade lists are of hybrid origin.

Pot new bulbs in January, choosing a pot size to leave no more than ¾ in. width of soil between the bulb and the pot rim. Bulbs should be planted to half their depth, in a mixture of 2 parts of loam and 1 part of sharp sand, plus a double handful of bonemeal to each bushel of the mixture. Start them into growth at a temperature of 60°F. As flower spikes appear, within about 3 weeks of being started, the temperature can rise to 65-70°F by day, with a night minimum of 60°F. Keep the plants well watered and fed with liquid fertilizer while

growing, maintaining a humid atmosphere. Remove dead flower heads if seed is not required. Gradually reduce the water supply from July to September (according to the time the bulbs were started into growth) until the pots are stored dry in a minimum temperature of 40°F for winter. Examine and repot as necessary in January, removing all dead roots. Renew the surface soil around the the bulbs not repotted, and start them into growth.

Young plants raised from seed should not be dried off for the winter until after their first flowering, but will need less water while the older bulbs are resting. Sow seed as soon as it is ripe, in a temperature of 50-66°F. Grow in quantities in large pots or boxes until plants are about 6 in. tall, then pot them individually into 4 in. pots for their first flowering.

Saintpaulia African violets are great favorites. The plants flower practically without stopping. The plants like a light soil mixture and that generally used is 3 parts of peat, 1 part of loam and 1 part of sharp sand. The plants do well in soilless composts. Saintpaulias have a small root system and rarely require beyond a 5 in. pot. For this plant plastic pots are more satisfactory than clay pots. The other requisites for the plants are shade, warmth and a moist atmosphere. This latter is not easy to provide in homes. The plants themselves do not take great quantities of water, but this should always be given at the same temperature. The best temperature appears to be 60°F but provided it is not too cold or too warm, the exact temperature does not seem to matter as much as seeing that this temperature is always maintained. Waterings where the temperature fluctuates will cause the appearance of unsightly white blotches on the leaves. The temperature should ideally be 55°F at night, and 70°F during the daytime, and if this can be kept going throughout the year the plants will do particularly well.

1 Leaf cuttings from a Saintpaulia
2 Use a small pot and sandy compost
3 and 4 The cutting and the new plant
5 A selection of pelargoniums. *Top, left to right* "Verona", "A Happy Thought", "Distinction". *Center, left to right* "Mrs. Parker", "Henry Cox", "Wilhelm Ian Guth", "Marechal Macmahon". *Below, left to right* "Mrs. Mappin", "Harry Hieover", "Flower of Spring" "Black Douglas"

Hippeastrum can be increased by offsets removed and potted separately when the plants are repotted in January

You get better plants ultimately if you prevent young saintpaulias from flowering. Pick off the buds until the plant reaches a larger size

However, this is not always possible and lower readings will slow down growth, but will not cause any damage, provided that the temperature does not fall for long below 50°F. When temperatures are low the soil should be kept rather dry and the atmosphere should also not be too moist. Established plants should be fertilized at intervals between April and October. Between November and mid-February in the greenhouse, no shading is necessary, but after this date the sun gets intense and light shading should be supplied. This is a good time for doing any potting that may be necessary.

There must be more **Pelargoniums** grown on window sills than any other plant. And there is such a wonderful variety. You can have many colors in the zonal types (these also have banded leaves from which they take their name), ornamental leaves with many variegations, scented leaves, double and single flowers and the pansy-faced kinds or regal pelargoniums.

In general pelargoniums grown in pots will do well in potting composts, though it is advisable to add a little extra lime to neutralize the acidity of the peat. Alternatively, particularly for potting rooted cuttings, a suitable soil mixture consists of 2 parts of good loam, 1 part of sand, 1 part of peat, all

parts by bulk, plus 1 cupful of ground limestone per bushel of the mixture. The ingredients should be throughly mixed and then watered with a liquid fertilizer with a high potash content. Some growers have been successful with the "no-soil" composts (peat/sand mixtures plus balanced fertilizers), while others use ordinary good garden soil which has been sterilized to kill harmful soil organisms.

Pelargoniums should never be over-potted. When repotting becomes necessary it is often possible, by removing the soil and slightly reducing the size of the root-ball, to repot into pots of the same size; otherwise the plants should be moved into pots one size larger only. They should always bepotted firmly.

Although plants should be watered freely during the growing period, in spring and summer, they should never be over-watered. The soil mixture should be free-draining so that surplus moisture can get away quickly, otherwise various root-rots and stem-rots may be encouraged. In winter plants will need little water, though the soil in the pots should not be allowed to dry out.

To keep plants growing freely and to maintain good leaf color it is necessary to fertilize them during the growing season.

Regular weak applications of proprietary liquid fertilizer should be given from about a month after the plants are in their final pots, until September. It should be noted, however, that plants in the fancy-leaved group should either not be fertilized at all, or the fertilizer they are given should not contain nitrogen. These kinds should, in any case, be given less water than others.

A number of zonal varieties can be induced to flower in winter, when blooms are always welcome. The method is to take cuttings in the spring. The young plants are grown during the summer and all flower buds are removed until late September. Plants treated in this way should flower throughout the winter months. It is best to maintain a minimum temperature of 60°F and the plants should be given as much light as possible. During the summer the plants may be placed in a sunny cold frame or the pots may be plunged in a sunny, sheltered place out of doors. They should be brought into the greenhouse in September.

Propagation of regal pelargoniums is by cuttings, which, like those of the other types, root easily. They should be about 3 in. long, taken from the top of the lateral shoots. They are trimmed back to a node and the bottom leaves are removed. They

1 *Saintpaulia lonantha* has
cultivars in a wide variety of
flower colors
2 *Vallota speciosa*, a bulbous
plant from South Africa, has
funnel-shaped, scarlet red flowers
3 This hippeastrum is a typical
example of a bicolored flower
4 Pelargonium "Carisbrooke" has
soft rose-pink petals with darker
markings
5 The white flowers of
pelargonium "Muriel Harris" are
feathered with red
6 Pelargonium "Black Prince"

will root quickly in a sterile rooting compost, in pots or in a propagating frame in
the greenhouse. Bottom heat is not required. Cuttings of this type are usually
taken in July or August.

Plants which are to be used for summer
bedding purposes are raised from cuttings
taken in August or September, rooting several in each 5-in. pot, or in boxes, spacing
the cuttings 2 in. apart. In February the
rooted cuttings are potted into individual 3
in. pots and kept in a temperature of 45-50°F
until April. They are then hardened off in a
cold frame before planting them out of
doors in late May or early June, when
danger of frost is over. Do not plant shal-
lowly; it is best to dig a hole large enough
and deep enough to take the plant up to its
first pair of leaves. Leggy plants may be
planted more deeply. Remove dead leaves
and flowers as soon as they are seen and
pinch out long, unwanted shoots from time
to time to keep the plants bushy. Keep the
plants well watered in dry weather. A gentle overhead spray in the evenings in hot
weather is beneficial. In September, before
the first frosts, the plants should be lifted

True geraniums are the hardy herbaceous summer-flowering plants that grow in rock gardens and borders. Pelargoniums are hardy only in very sheltered districts.

Leaves of the scented species of pelargoniums when added to sponge cakes and fruit jellies gives them distinctive flavors

and brought into the greenhouse for the winter. The shoots should be cut back, long roots trimmed and the plants potted into small pots. The minimum winter temperature in the greenhouse should be around 42°F.

Vallota (val-lo-ta)

A genus of one species, a bulbous plant from Cape Province, South Africa. It is commonly known as Scarborough lily. It is not reliably hard, but is an admirable pot plant for a sunny window sill. *V. speciosa* (syn. *V. purpurea*) reaches 1-2 ft., and has broad leaves, to 18 in. long and erect stems bearing up to 10 large, funnel-shaped, glowing scarlet-red flowers in August and September; there is a white variety, *alba*, and other varieties have been recorded.

The bulbs are best potted in July in a compost of equal parts of fibrous loam, leafmold and sharp sand. The tip of the large bulb should be just below the surface and potted firmly. Do not repot for several years, but fertilize regularly while the bulbs are growing, before flowering. Ample water is required during the growing season, but the soil should be kept nearly dry while the plants are dormant, after the leaves die down. Propagation is by offsets removed when repotting.

Offset

This is a term commonly used for a young plant which can be detached from the parent plant and thus forms an easy means of propagation.

Leaf cuttings Healthy, well-developed leaves of numerous plants provide a useful means of propagation. Those that root particularly easily by this means include various begonias, such as *Begonia rex*, gloxinias, saintpaulias, streptocarpus, and some ferns. After removing a leaf from the parent plant make a few light incisions with a sharp knife across the veins on the underside and then lay the leaf on the surface of moist compost, consisting of peat and sharp sand. Peg the leaf down gently; hairpins are useful for this purpose. Leaf cuttings should be shaded from direct sunlight and have a reasonably warm and moist atmosphere. Begonia leaves, among others, will produce roots quite quickly, even when just placed in a saucer of water.

4

5

6

CHAPTER FIFTEEN

HOUSE PLANTS

The type of heating that you use and the temperatures you maintain in your various rooms during the winter will affect the types of plant you can grow. Some plants, notably begonias, are very intolerant of gas fumes, so that if your homes are heated by gas, you may not be able to grow begonias satisfactorily. If you have really warm rooms, maintaining, perhaps, an average temperature of 70°F, they will be far too warm for such plants as ivy or × *Fatshedera lizei*. With high temperatures such as these, the plants will continue growing during the winter and more water will be required. The winter growth may not be very ornamental, as the lack of light will prevent the formation of good size leaves.

The highest temperatures are around midday, but many rooms are kept cold during the day, when people are out at work, warm in the evening, when everyone is at home, but cool off during the late evening and the early morning after people have gone to bed.

Such a contradiction of natural rhythm is sufficient to disturb any plant and it is easy to see that keeping plants in good condition in the winter is less simple in the house than in a greenhouse. If you have some system of central heating, the problem is comparatively simple, but for rooms with only sporadic warmth, the matter is less straightforward. However, there are house plants to suit all conditions.

It is fairly safe to say that no plant will tolerate the conditions that are to be found on a mantelpiece above a fire. The atmosphere is far too dry and the alternations of cold and heat are too much for some plants, except the toughest succulents. Even if the temperature is equable, plants that are put too near the window risk being chilled, or even frosted, when the weather is very cold, and they should be moved farther into the room during these periods.

Even when the temperature is satisfactory, the dry atmosphere is not beneficial to plants. This, however, can easily be overcome, by placing the pots in a larger container and filling this container with some moisture-retentive material. Peat is most frequently used, but moss or vermiculite does equally well. Some people get perfectly satisfactory results with damp newspaper, which is topped with moss to look more elegant. By these means one can maintain a moist atmosphere in the immediate surroundings of the plant without affecting the correct state of moisture of the soil ball.

1 The lavender-blue flowers and persistent pink bracts of *Aechmea rhodocyanea*, a tough house plant
2 *Maranta mackoyana* must be protected from sunlight to keep its leaf color
3 *Ficus elastica variegata*, the Indiarubber Plant, a good room plant, it also valuable for greenhouse decoration
4 *Philodendron scandens*

More house plants are killed by overwatering than by any other cause. Plants cannot live without water, but they can be drowned. Plants need water most when they are making growth. This is usually during the spring and summer.

When to give water is only satisfactorily learned by experience, but the following rules are generally acceptable.

1 When water is applied, it should be in sufficient quantity to moisten the whole of the soil ball. The water should be at room temperature. Rain water is preferable but not essential.

2 The soil should be allowed to dry out between waterings. This is not too easy to in-

1 A group of flowering house
plants, all of which add color
indoors in winter
2 The arrow-shaped leaves of
Philodendron hastatum need
frequent cleaning
3 TheWatermelon Plant,
peperomia sandersii
4 A collection of house plants
which includes *(Back left to
right) hedera canariensis, ficus
elastica* Sansevieria. *(Front, left
to right)* croton, dieffenbachia,
begonia masoniana, maranta,
peperomia and aphelandra

terpret. We do not want the soil to become
dust dry, but on the other hand, we want to
avoid saturation. A useful rule of thumb
with clay pots and soil mixtures, is to strike
the side of the pot with your knuckle. If the
resultant sound is dull, watering is not
needed, but if it is a ringing sound, water
should be applied. With peat mixtures the
weight of the pot is a more reliable indication. If it feels light, water is wanted, but not
if it feels heavy. The same applies, but to a
lesser extent, with soil mixtures in plastic
pots. These are more difficult to gauge.
3 During cold weather plants make little or
no growth, and so require less water.
Growth is also slowed down when there is
little light. It is safe, therefore, during the
winter to keep all watering down to a
minimum, even though the room may be
kept at quite a high temperature. Naturally,
plants in warm rooms will require more
than those in cool surroundings.
4 From about mid-April it is probable that

If a plant is making new leaves and stems it is almost certain also to be making new roots

If the soil is too wet the roots may decline and rot unless the soil dries out quickly

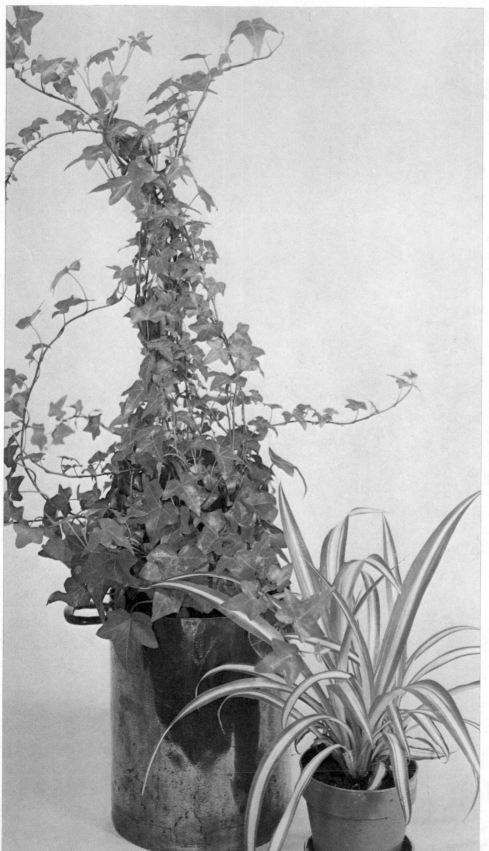

growth will start, and so more water may be required. Be cautious, nevertheless, until you see new leaves appearing. It is possible to knock the plant out of its pot to see if new roots (characterized by their white tips) are forming and to replace the soil ball without disturbance. When growth is vigorous water will be needed more frequently. Topping checks growth temporarily and watering should be on a reduced scale until a resumption of growth is seen.

5 By the end of August it is advisable to discourage much further growth and encourage the plant to mature its new growth. This is done by keeping the plant as dry as possible.

6 The type of leaf will give some indication of the plant's requirements. Plants with thick leaves or with succulent leaves (such

Dusty leaves inhibit growth. Clean them often with a soft tissue and clean water

The leaves of bromeliads such as aechmea and neoregelia form a "vase". Water these plants by keeping this filled with water, preferably rain, to keep deposits from forming on the leaves

as the large-leaved ficus and sansevieria) can tolerate longer periods without water than thin-leaved plants. These latter will probably wilt when they become too dry and they should be watered at once. The thicker leaved plants will not wilt and so should be inspected frequently. Drought, unless acute, will not kill them but may cause subsequent leaf drop.

If leaves turn yellow and fall off, it usually indicates over-watering. However some plants, such as *Ficus benjamina,* will naturally shed their year-old leaves in the autumn and most plants shed a few leaves in the couse of the year. Excessive defoliation is almost certainly due to incorrect watering; although it can be caused by under-watering as well as by over-watering. If the plant becomes unsteady in the pot, this is generally due to root-rot caused by excessive water and is very difficult to arrest. Some leaves will wilt in the summer if they are in direct sunlight. If the soil appears to be satisfactorily moist, a syringeing of the leaves with water will generally restore them to their normal turgidity, and in any case, they will resume their normal appearance as soon as the sunlight goes.

During the summer, when growth is most vigorous, the plants may be fertilized.

3

1 *Hedera helix* "Chicago", a pointed-leaved ivy with *(front) Chlorophytum capense,* sometimes known as the Spider Plant
2 The poinsettia, *Euphorbia pulcherrima*
3 A young plant of *Tetrastigma voineriana*
4 *Sansevieria trifasciata laurentii,* and Hedera "Heiss" in the foreground
5 *Scindapsus aureus,* the Devil's Ivy
6 The deeply cut leaves of *Philodendron elegans* are an attractive addition to any collection of indoor plants

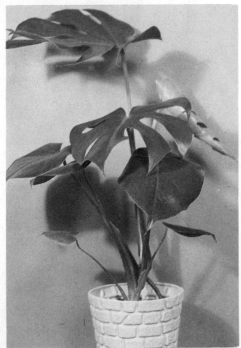

4

5

6

A liquid fertilizer is most easily applied and should be given according to the instructions. Little and often is invariably better than doses in excess of those recommended. Unless the plant is well-rooted, feeding should not be applied and is not necessary for plants that have been repotted. Repotting is done in the early summer. Plants are usually potted into a pot one size larger. Plants from 5-in. pots are put into 6-in. pots and so on. The only exception is that the 4-in. pot is very rarely used and plants are moved from 3-in. to 5-in. pots. Plants with very thin roots such as begonias and peperomias do better in a mixture of 2 parts of leafmold to 1 part of sharp sand, while epiphytes, such as the bromeliads, are usually given a mixture of peat, leafmold and sharp sand. However, it is only rarely epiphytes require any shifting, as they use the soil as an anchorage only. After being potted the plants should be kept on the dry side until the roots have penetrated the new soil. It is best to move plants from 2 in. pots to 5-in. pots after a year, as the 3-in. pots dry out so quickly, but after that most house plants will need repotting only every other year. The second year the plant will need feeding.

1 *Sansevieria trifasciata laurentii,*
2 A collection of ferns in a bark container, with helxine added in the front
3 *Dracaena godseffiana* has opposite leaves heavily spotted with cream and likes a warm room with plenty of light
4 The striped dracaena produces whorls of green leaves, edged and heavily marked with cream
5 *Dieffenbachia amoena,* called Dumb Cane. Poisonous when eaten
6 *Dracaena massangeana,* a spreading plant with variegated leaves.
7 Evergreen plants provide interest all the year aound. Many have attractive leaves like this *Fittonia argyroneura*

Climbing aeroids like philodendron, syngonium and scindapsus will grow more luxuriantly if they are encouraged to climb a "pole" such as one made of wire netting stuffed with damp moss

The darker the green and the thicker the leaf the more tolerant the plant will be of shady conditions. You can grow these plants away from the window

5

6

7

CHAPTER SIXTEEN

BOTTLE GARDENS

Once you have grown house plants inside a bottle you will always be enchanted with this form of captive gardening. My own bottle gardens consist of two carboys, two outsize brandy snifters and an outsize storage jar. But I have made them in many other vessels. Naturally the wider the mouth of the bottle the easier it is to plant it, but if it is very wide you may need a lid or stopper.

The success of this type of gardening depends on the creation of an isolated microclimate inside the vessel and on giving it plenty of light.

Most leafy plants from warm countries need, in cultivation, not only heat but humidity. This vital component of growth is the most difficult for the amateur to understand, because it is invisible and not readily discernible.

In a greenhouse, humidity or air moisture is provided by "damping down" the floor, benches, or both. But when we come to cultivate these plants in rooms, air dryness becomes a serious problem, because all our methods of room heating tend to dry out the air.

To enclose room plants within glass was a logical step, and from 1840 or until the beginning of this century, Wardian Cases — so-called after their originator, Dr. Nathaniel Ward — were a feature of many Victorian homes.

Wardian Case

Nathaniel Ward (1791-1868), a London doctor and naturalist, accidentally discovered the plant-growing case named after him. Wishing to study a chrysalis he brought back from the countryside he buried it in some soil in an almost airtight glass jar. He noticed that seeds in the soil soon began to germinate, forming plants which grew vigorously. He continued making experiments and in 1838 he made the first Wardian case from metal and glass. It was soon used to make fern cases in which moisture-loving ferns could be grown indoors inside the case in spite of a dry surrounding atmosphere. It also enabled living plants to be dispatched successfully over long distances when transport was slow and often difficult. It was used by Robert Fortune when he made his plant-collecting expedition to China in 1845. Later, it made possible the introduction of tea plants to India, the worldwide distribution of quinine-producing plants and the first cultivation of bananas outside China.

Apart from such practical uses, the Wardian Case became unfashionable early in this century and few remain in existence. During the 1940s, in the U.S.A., the same

principle was applied to an indoor gardener's "gimmick" — growing plants in a bottle.

The standard bottle for gardening is the large, round, 10-gallon carboy, which until recently was used for acid and distilled water. Oval carboys and the vertical-sided demijohn used for spirits are also attractive. In fact any bottle can be used as long as its aperture is large enough to allow plants to be inserted.

Bottling plants is much easier than the final result may lead one to imagine — certainly simpler than putting a ship in a bottle! After cleaning the bottle thoroughly, add a 1-in. deep layer of fine gravel. This is followed by soil, which can be poured in through a paper funnel or a cardboard tube

to avoid soiling the glass. A good mixture consists of 1 part of fibrous loam, 2 parts of peat and 1 part of coarse sand. The soil mixture should be just damp, by no means wet, and the soil layer should be 5—6 in. deep depending on the size of the bottle.

The only tools needed are a cane with a spool pushed firmly on to one end and a length of 1-in.-wide wooden lath, pointed at one end. Small plastic tools, a "spade" at one end, a "fork" or "rake" at the other, are sold for use by indoor gardeners. If these are cut in half and the cut ends pushed into lengths of cane, two useful tools can be made for use when the bottle is being prepared and planted. With the spool the soil is firmed down; the flat end of the lath is used to push the soil about and the pointed end

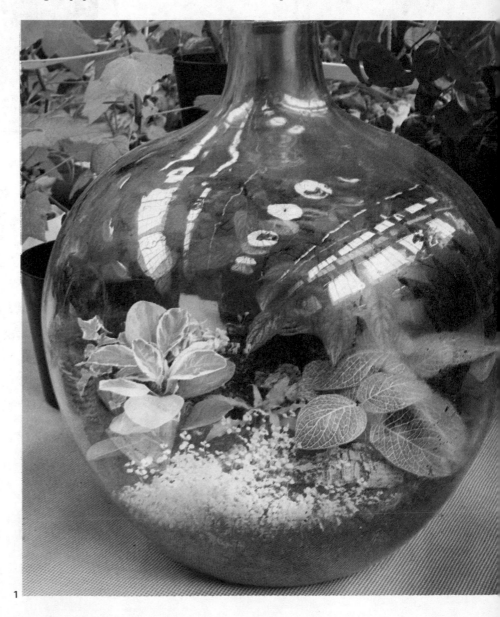

1

to excavate planting holes. It is essential to make each hole large enough to accommodate the roots of the plant destined for it. It may benecessary to take some soil off the root ball before it can be passed through the neck of the bottle.

Start with the plants around the outside of the bottle (to avoid dropping soil on those already planted). Push the root ball through the aperture, then hold the plant by its leaves, push it gently through, and let it drop. It can then be pushed into its hole with the cane and lath (or with the plastic tools), the roots covered with soil, and the spool used to make the plant firm.

Little attention is needed once the bottle garden is planted. If the top is kept on, little or no water is needed, but condensation will form on the glass at certain times; this gradually clears as the moisture runs down the inside of the glass into the soil. This is, in fact, a continual cycle; water given off through the leaves of the plants in the form of vapor condenses on the glass, runs back into the soil, is absorbed again through the roots of the plants and is again given off through the foliage. If the bottle is open, a cupful of water every month or so in summer is desirable. Dead leaves are removed

1 A variety of plants lend themselves to being grown in a bottle garden and they need little attention after they have been planted. Small specimens can be bought for this purpose
2 A nineteenth-century example of a Wardian case, from which the bottle garden developed

by cutting them with a piece of razorblade wired to a cane; they can then be lifted out on a pointed cane. Keep the bottle out of direct sunlight, but make sure that it is in good indirect light.

Exactly the same principles, but less trouble, can be used if it is desired to plant a large goldfish bowl, a brandy glass or a wide-necked jar.

Plants should be purchased in the smallest pots available. Suitable plants are: *Calathea oppenheimiana, C. ornata, C. zebrina; Cryptanthus bivittatus, C. tricolor* and others; *Fittonia argyroneura, F. verschaffeltii; Maranta leuconeura kerchoveana, M. massangeana, M. makoyana; Neanthe bella; Peperomia magnoliaefolia, P. caperata, P. hederaefolia, P. sandersii* and *Vriesia splendens.* Ferns such as *Asplenium nidus* and *Pellaea rotundifolia* are suitable. Rampant growers such as tradescantia must be avoided, and flowering plants are more trouble than they are worth.

In one of my wide-necked jars I have sloped the soil, arranged an attractive piece of rock on the summit and planted **Nertera** which covers the soil. This is a charming little plant. There is one species in cultivation, *N. depressa.* It is a low-growing, spreading plant, its main decorative feature being its dense crop of bright orange, pea-size berries. Coming from New Zealand, Australia and South America, it is almost hardy and is sometimes grown on rock gardens, with winter protection.

Nertera is normally grown as a greenhouse pot plant, in sandy compost, such as 2 parts of sandy loam, 1 part each of sand and leafmold. Plants should be shaded from strong sunlight. Pot in spring in warmth and afterward, when the plants are established, move the pots to a cool place to assist flower and berry formation. Keep the plants well watered. Out of doors they may be grown on shady parts of the rock garden in light rich soil, but will need protection in winter. They are easily raised from seed sown in spring or may be increased by potting small pieces separated from established plants.

One of my carboys contains ferns and

these look extremely attractive seen through glass. Most gardeners like ferns, but usually the atmosphere in a home is too dry for them. A bottle garden suits them well and you can find many pretty little species.

For bottle gardens, lower ferns into place when they are quite tiny. You will find it easy to prick them into the soil.

Propagation In spring when the ferns are repotted and just as new growth begins to swell, a plant can be divided and the divisions potted up separately.

Some ferns, for example Aspidium, occasionally produce small plants on the fronds. These can be pegged down into pots or boxes of fine compost and severed after rooting has taken place.

The most interesting method of propagation is by sowing the spores that are produced in the spore cases (sporangia) on the backs of the fronds. Put a mature frond into a white envelope for a few days to dry off, and collect the powdery spores. Sow these on the surface of sandy compost, previously sterilized, in a pan first half filled with crocks. Stand the pan in shallow water, cover it with glass, and shade. Autumn sowing is best but the spores may be saved until the spring. The resulting green plant, or prothallus, bears no resemblance to the original fern but is the sexual generation in the life cycle of the fern. The prothalli should be put into a pan or box about 1 in. apart, just pressed on to the soil, and the resulting tiny fern plants potted up individually, once they are big enough to handle.

Cryptanthus *(krip-tan-thus)*

Sometimes called "earth stars", an allusion to their starfish-like shapes. A small genus of dwarf, tufted, spiny plants from Brazil, suitable as house plants. The flowers are mostly white, and borne in a dense tuft of bracts in the center of the rosette.

Stolons are produced in the outer leaf axils, making offsets which can be removed for propagation. When grown as house plants they should be kept nearly dry in winter. In the house they need a light position; the smaller kinds are suitable for growing in bottle gardens.

CHAPTER SEVENTEEN
FLOWER ARRANGEMENT

Floral decorations should be designed to suit their surroundings and although an oriental-styled arrangement might well suit a living room or, if it is designed on a large scale, the more spacious classroom and conference hall, it is generally not suited to large or more ornate interiors. Here, most of the flowers have to compete with colored, even patterned furnishings and walls, and so it follows that to be noticeable the arrangements must be large as well as colorful.

In general, there are two great divisions of styles; one in which the accent is on line, silhouette and/or design, and the other in which color is the dominant feature and in which the mass tends to be set inside a certain outline.

Modern schools But since flower arrangement is such a personal art, it is also fluid and ever-changing and so we have many variations on these themes. At times the two are joined and we see a contemporary style which is an amalgam of line and mass.

Universally, the term "flower arrangement" is more comprehensive than at first might appear. By "flower" we mean any type of plant material and, paradoxical though it may be, many arrangements are made without a true flower as part of it. Obviously, leaves and branches, blossom and berries form a part of many flower ar-

2

3

1

4

Cut the firm edge from wire netting. It will then be more malleable

To fix candles on pinholders first warm the pinholder. Use the same method to remove the candle

7

rangements as one would expect, but perhaps not so obviously, so do bare branches, driftwood, stems, roots, seed pods, grasses and all kinds of fruiting parts of plants as well as fungi, lichens, mosses and even seaweeds.

Containers to use The same liberal attitude is adopted by the modern flower arranger toward containers. For centuries flower vases have tended to be things apart, vessels designed only to support and display flowers. But for the modern imaginative flower arranger, anything goes — so long as it can be made to hold water or some water-retentive material and is suitable for the flowers, setting and occasion.

There are exceptions, of course. For example, period arrangements ought to be made not only in the style known to be fashionable at the time in question but also

in vessels of the period. Alternatively, faithful reproductions can be used. Unless this is done, one never captures the true flavor of the period. They ought also, and for the same reason, to contain flowers grown and known at the same time.

Japanese flower arrangement Centuries ago, the Japanese devised sophisticated ways of anchoring stems which meant that the old, massed Rikkwa style was dropped in favor of arrangements in which stems could be

1 A bottle is used for a long-lasting arrangement of achillea, rushes, yucca seed heads and mahonia leaves. Gourds are wired into place
2 Chicken netting is crushed to form a base of any shape or size. Green Oasis hold stems

firmly and keep blooms fresh. Pinholders held by Plasticine fit firmly in the bottom of containers
3 A white arrangement for the center of a table. The first central stem is put in vertically to define the height and is the pivot from which the stems will appear to radiate
4 The stems of stocks determine the width of the arrangement, and intermediate stems are neither higher nor longer than the first stems
5 Some of the larger flowers, viburnum, should be recessed to hide the holder as well as to provide depth and interest to the contour
6 The rose buds, which will open wide, are added last, to the arrangement. This arrangement provides a delightful effect for the center of a table
7 Beech leaves and chrysanthemums

1

2

held just as the arranger required. These then became more and more stylized. As they were originally linked with religion in some form or another, Japanese flower arrangement continued down through the centuries to be linked with religious symbolism or spiritual interpretations.

The three main stems were given greatest importance and were shown to signify Heaven, Man and Earth. But this attitude should not deter the severely practical minded because the proportions of these stems are of such practical and logical beauty that they can be followed easily and with pleasing results. Furthermore, the mystical Japanese flower arrangement has now been digested and revised in the form of Ikebana, possibly the most universally

popular form of simple flower arrangement at this time.

Patterns for designs Because the materials used are so diverse, it is unlikely that one would ever see a flower arrangement exactly like another, but it is possible to see many that look alike and are made in the same style or pattern. This is mainly because it is the purpose of flower arrangement to display each flower to advantage and we find that a certain number of stems tend to fall into certain styles, mainly pyramidal or conical — even if a definite pattern was not the original intention. This is particularly the case when uniform flowers have to be arranged.

Choice of containers Although beauty is the goal, one's aim should be practical also.

Flower arrangements not only need to suit their surroundings but also their containers, so that vessel and contents make a unit. Flowers which are long stemmed and heavy need anchoring well. In a container which is too small for them they may overbalance. Some flowers absorb more water than others and so need a deep vessel. Choice of container is vitally important. Not only must it hold the flowers well but it needs also to match the mood, suit the color, texture and style of the contents.

Keeping flowers fresh Since flowers are brought indoors to enjoy, it follows that they should be kept alive as long as possible. The most important factor for lasting freshness is that all materials should be hardened properly. All should be turgid

Like most of their kind lilies can be cut and arranged while the buds are just colored. They will then open slowly in water

Many flowers will take water in much more easily if most of the foilage is first removed

1 and 2 An example of Ikebana. The longest stem symbolizes Heaven. The second longest represents Man, and the shortest stem, Earth
3 Another arrangement. The central spray of *Viburnum opulus* is arranged to form the skeleton
4 A third-dimensional effect is added by the low stems in front
5 The final arrangement with alstroemerias, carnations and euphorbia

and taking water properly before arrangement. This means that as soon as possible after they are gathered, stems should be placed in deep water, covering any foliage on the stems should this be present, for at least an hour, longer if possible. By covering the leaves with water in this way, respiration is prevented and the stem will become turgid more quickly than if it had been allowed to function naturally.

To ensure quick intake of water, all but hollow and very fleshy stems should be split at the base upward for ½ in. or more according to the length of stem. This exposes the soft inner tissues. It also expels any air present which tends to cause a lock in the stem tissues and prevents water being drawn up. To prevent flowers from wilting, it is advisable that the water into which they are placed should be warmed to 100—110°F.

Hardening and preparing materials Some plant material once cut from the plant cannot take water easily; acacia or mimosa, for example, very little. Only humidity around the flowers and leaves keeps them fresh. You can, for instance, keep mimosa fluffy for days, even weeks, if you place it under a glass dome.

Those stems which exude a milky juice or latex, for example euphorbias, cannot take water until the latex coagulates. The easiest way to effect this is to singe the cut stem ends over a flame as soon as possible after cutting. Any stems which are shortened for arrangement after the singed stems have been given a deep drink should be re-singed.

Any flower which fails to become turgid — hollyhocks are examples — and all young and immature foliage, whether individual leaves or branches, should have the stems in an inch or two of boiling water until turgid. The stem ends thus treated often become blackened and sometimes soft. Once it has become turgid, this portion may be cut away and if the stem has to be shortened for arrangement there should be no need to treat the new cut end.

Preservatives and nutrients Certain preservatives and nutrients help to maintain freshness. There are several proprietary brands on sale, most of which contain some glucose which seems to be appreciated by most flowers.

In arrangements of fresh shrub and tree materials, such as blossoms in bud or Christmas evergreens expected to stand for some weeks, use a little of any good soluble plant food, sufficient to make a very weak solution.

There is some validity in the use of a copper coin in the water within a container. These discourage or delay bacterial action. There is also less bacterial activity in metal containers. On the other hand, water in glass containers, especially if placed in sunlight, tends to become foul.

Always strip the leaves from the portion of stem which is to remain under water and avoid hammering or crushing woody and fibrous stems. The foamed urea plastic stemholders, such as Oasis and Florapak, contain formaldehyde which is a form of disinfectant and these help keep flowers fresh.

Holding stems firmly in place If the flower arrangement is to be quick and easy as well as effective it must be possible for the gardener to place any stem at will and to be quite confident that it is well anchored. One of the most versatile of stemholders is large mesh, 1½—2 in. wire-netting. It is also possible to buy plastic-covered netting in flower shops and other places. This is quite good, especially when vases must not be scratched, but is not quite so malleable as the common kind. Large mesh is the most malleable and will give under the pressure of a thick stem being pushed through a crumpled mass. Small mesh on the other hand, is too rigid and so prevents arrangement. It is best to use the large mesh even

1

2

Foundations for cones and other shapes can be bought ready formed. Use them dry for dried materials

When making all-foliage arrangements look for contrasting shapes as well as textures and colors

for small containers. Miniature arrangements, obviously need other treatment.

Most often it is best to fill the container from rim to base with a mass of crumpled netting, first cut just a fraction wider than the greatest diameter and twice the depth of the container. If the netting is first folded into a U shape and then squashed into the container with the cut ends uppermost, some of these cut ends may then be hooked over the rim to hold the netting firm. Sometimes netting slips in highly glazed containers.

If very large or outsize arrangements are being planned it is advisable to use more wire-netting than usual and to allow this to protrude well above the rim of the vase. It will then help to support very tall stems.

Arrangement is always easier when the netting fills the container from rim to base because then the bases of long stems are firmly held. However, this is unsightly when glass containers are used. In this case a small crumpled piece of netting should be fixed in the mouth of the container so that the stems will pass through it into the water. Low-hanging materials will hide the lower part of the netting.

Lightweight containers may be half filled with sand to weight the base, with netting arranged on top.

Excellent modern alternatives to wire netting are the water-retentive foamed urea stemholders, such as Florapak. Because these hold, but do not spill water, they are useful for arrangements on polished furniture. They are also useful for arrangements which have to be transported and those to be out of reach where they cannot be topped up daily. These can be used either to fill the vase from rim to base or, alternatively, they can be used at the base of a container with wire netting arranged at the higher level near the rim.

One great advantage is that only a small portion of stem end need be inserted into the plastic which means that comparatively short stems can be used in tall arrangements.

Other plastics, Oasis for instance, evaporate quite quickly and have to be moistened daily but their great value lies in the fact that they do not quickly disintegrate and so may safely be used ex-container — in a saucer for example. Water poured into the saucer will be taken up by capillary action.

Pinholders Known as *kenzan* in Japan, pinholders are ancient stemholders brought up to date. They come in many sizes and shapes including minute examples for miniature arrangements or for holding a single flower. They are mostly used in shallow containers, but they are also sometimes useful at the base of a tall container, especially when a tall and heavy branch is to be displayed.

These holders consist of upright pin, needle or nail points projecting from a heavy metal base. Plastic pinholders are manufactured but these will not efficiently hold all types of stems. Stems are impaled on the points, either vertically or at an an-

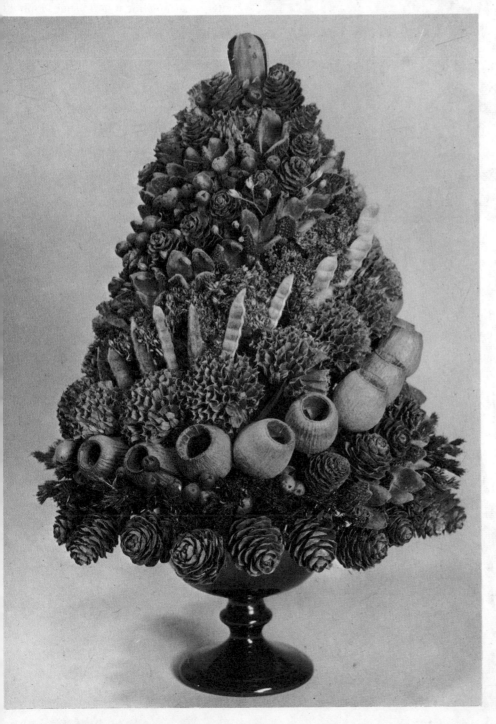

A free-style arrangement of foliage based on the sheaf form. Vine leaves add central color
2 A jug holds a late summer bouquet
3 Materials are mounted by short wire stems, on a shaped base of Oasis

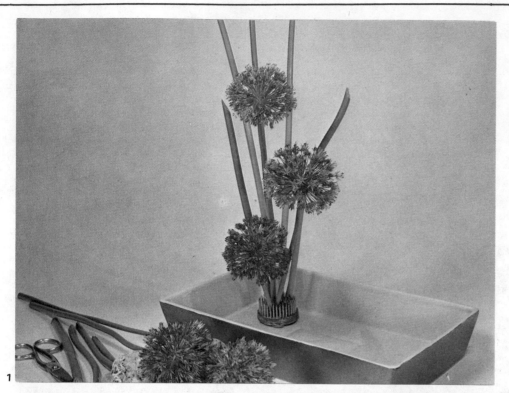

gle. Woody stems are more easily arranged if they are cut on a slant.

To prevent movement, the pinholder should be firmly anchored before arrangement takes place. This is simply done by making four or five small pills of plasticine which should be lightly attached to the dry base of the holder. If this is then pressed against the equally dry floor of the container the pills become squashed and it sticks.

No holders of any kind should ever show after an arrangement is finished. Pinholders are easy to hide by using large flowers placed low, but not actually touching the water, or leaves, stones, shells, driftwood and other objects, all of which should harmonize with the other components of the arrangement.

1 Alliums are cut short, and the stem retained for a line arrangement
2 Smooth stones hide the pinholder in the final clean effect
3 A white cherub vase holds dried flowers, wheat and pussy willow
4 Lily "Enchantment" in a vertical design for a modern bowl
5 Seeds heads of *Iris sibirica*, held by a pinholder, complete the arrangement
6 Leaves of the horse chestnut are a favored subject in spring
7 Gaillardias help toward a bold effect in a well arranged vase in summer

Round flowers, chrysanthemums
for instance, look well with spiky forms

Few flowers are really straight stemmed.
Look for the hint of a curve and exploit it

6

7

8

5

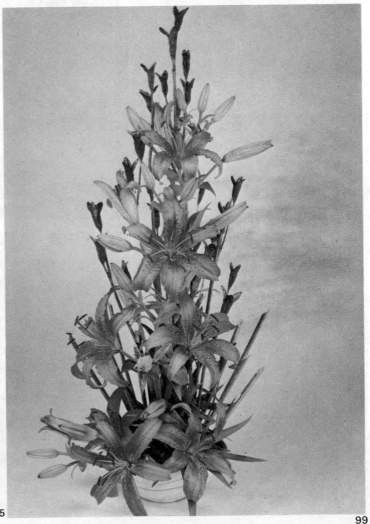

CHAPTER EIGHTEEN
FOLIAGE FOR CUTTING

A flower arranger needs all kinds of foliage and individual leaves to make home decorations throughout the year.

Many of the shrubs described in earlier chapters can be cut for use. There are also many perennials which are worth growing for their handsome leaves. Some also give lovely flowers.

Arum (a-rum)

It is thought the burning taste of these plants gave them the ancient name of arum from the Arabic *ar,* fire *(Araceae).* There are hardy and half-hardy perennials in this tuberous-rooted genus, grown for their showy spathes, spadices and foliage, the true flowers being insignificant.

Species cultivated *A. italicum,* 1½ ft., creamy white spathes, leaves appear in the autumn. Forms with spotted or marbled leaves such as var. *pictum,* are more showy, *A. maculatum,* the cuckoo-pint or lords and ladies, and many other names, 6 in., leaves plain green or dark spotted, spathes yellowish-green and spotted with purple. *A. pictum,* 1 ft., grown for its large light green leaves, spathes white within, margined with purple.

The species will thrive in any ordinary soil and prefer a shady spot.

Bergenia (ber-gen-i-a)

These hardy perennial herbaceous plants with large evergreen leaves were at one time included with the saxifrages. The flowers come in early spring and are showy in white, pink or red-purple, borne in large heads. The large leathery, glossy leaves are decorative, especially as in some kinds, the foliage is suffused with reddish color, in winter.

Cultivars "Ballawley Hybrid", 1½ ft., crimson flowers, dark purplish leaves in winter. "Delbees", 1 ft., leaves turn red in winter, flowers rosy, March-April. "Evening Glow", 15-18 in., dark purple flowers, reddish-bronze foliage. "Silberlicht" ("Silver Light"), 1 ft., flowers white flushed pink, spring. Others are available and more are likely to be seen in cultivation as time goes on.

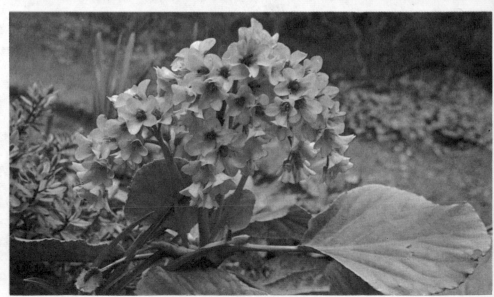

These members of the saxifrage family thrive in any soil, in sun or shade. However, to get full color of the winter leaves, it will be necessary to give the bergenias full sun exposure; and under those conditions they will also produce their flowers somewhat earlier.

Epimedium (ep-im-ee-de-um)

Decorative hardy perennials for the rock garden or wild garden. In the spring the small shield-shaped leaves are pale green with pink, rose and pale lemon tints. They become deeper green in the summer and are attractively veined; by the autumn they take on rich tints of deeper coloring. The light, arching sprays of flowers are borne in spring and early summer. There are many species in cultivation.

Plant in the autumn or spring in sandy loam enriched with leafmold or peat. Choose a cool shady border or rock garden. They do well under trees, provided the location is not too dry, where they retain their leaves throughout the winter. They are useful for suppressing weeds. Propagation is by division of the roots in the autumn.

Ruta (roo-ta)

The species in general cultivation is *R. graveolens*, known as rue or herb of grace and grown for centuries for its medicinal properties. It makes a half-woody evergreen shrub up to 3 ft. in height and width. The leaves are glaucous, 3-5 in. long and composed of many leaflets up to ½ in. long. Deep yellow, 4-petaled flowers, about ¾ in. wide are borne from July to September. "Jackman's Blue", 2 ft., is a most desirable compact form with deep glaucous-blue leaves against which the yellow flowers contrast effectively; var. *variegata*, 2½ ft., has leaves bordered with white.

Although the common rue may be confined to the herb garden, the cultivars in particular make handsome, dwarf shrubs when grown for effect in herbaceous or shrub borders. Fairly severe pruning of mature bushes is desirable in April at least every other year, in order to maintain a compact habit. Propagation is by seed sown in the spring or, by cuttings 4-6 in. long made from ripened side-shoots in late summer, rooted in a cold frame. The resultant plants may be moved to their final positions the following autumn.

Artemisia (ar-tem-ees-e-a)

A large genus, widely distributed over the world, of shrubs, sub-shrubs, herbaceous perennials and annuals, grown mainly for their dainty, aromatic foliage which is very finely cut in some species. The genus shows a great diversity of habit and leaf shape: the flowers are very small and are seldom of much account, though they are often borne in large panicles or plumes. The herb used for flavorings and tarragon vinegar is a member of this family. Most of the artemisias are sun lovers, but *A. lactiflora*, with its sprays of creamy white flowers, will grow in semishade and is a useful plant for the herbaceous border.

Annual species cultivated *A. sacrorum viridis*, summer fire, 4 ft., strictly a sub-shrub but grown as an annual.

Herbaceous and sub-shrubs *A. absinthium*, wormwood, 1½ ft., flowers yellow, summer. *A. dracunculus*, tarragon, 2 ft., whitish green. *A. gnaphalodes*, 2 ft., foliage grey-white. *A. lactiflora*, 4 ft., creamy white flowers in lumes, late summer.

Shrubs *A. abrotanum*, 3—4 ft., the southernwood, fragrant, grey, filigree foliage. *A. arborescens*, 3 ft., silvery foliage retained throughout the year. The flowers of both these shrubs, when provided, are insignificant. They are grown for their foliage.

Plant in autumn or spring in sunny borders in ordinary soil. Propagate shrubby species by summer cuttings and herbaceous by cuttings or division. Seed may be sown in spring of annual and herbaceous species.

Brassicas The beautiful ornamental cabbage and kale are at their best during the fall season when flowers are scarce.

The crinkled leaves are most effective when used with arrangements in a vase and the plants are also colorful and long lasting in the garden. The plants are easily raised from seed which are obtainable as variegated silver, variegated purple and variegated mixed. Sow the seed in April or May and transplant the seedlings about 18 in. apart. Cultivation is the same as for ordinary cabbage.

Hosta Plaintain lily. Hardy herbaceous plants, natives of E. Asia, principally Japan,

1 *Arum maculatum*

2 *Bergenia purpurascens* bears its purplish flowers in June whereas

3 *Bergenia cordifolia* is one of the earliest hardy perennials to flower, producing its pink blooms in March

4 *Epimedium niveum* in flower

5 *Epimedium versicolor*, grown for its ornamental foliage

5

4

valued for their large decorative leaves in variable greens, some glaucous, some with variegated patterns in green, silver and gold. Their flower racemes carry tubular, lily-like blooms mainly in summer, in shades purple-lilac or white. Preferring partial shade, hostas are ideal for mass planting in woodland settings or other shady places. Used in clumps they discourage weeds from establishing in border edges where they make bold contrast with taller growing plants. As moisture-loving plants they are excellent for planting by streams or on the banks of ponds. When grown in pots or tubs and watered adequately, hostas are fine for use in terrace or patio gardening, or in greenhouses and conservatories. Their leaves and flowers last well in water and are used widely in floral arrangements.

Species cultivated *H. lancifolia albomarginata*, 1 ft., leaves with a narrow white border, flowers violet. *H. fortunei marginato-alba*, 2 ft., large leaves with a broad pure white border, flowers pale lilac. *H. decorata*, broad oval leaves, narrowly edged with white, flower stems to 2 ft.,

flowers dark violet. *H. fortunei*, 2 ft., broad glaucous green leaves, flowers pale lilac; var. *albo-picta*, leaves yellowish-white darkening later with a green edge. *H. lancifolia*, 1½ ft., narrow, dark green leaves, flowers pale lilac. *H. plantaginea*, 1½ ft., large glossy, green leaves, flowers white, fragrant, early autumn. *H rectifolia*, 1½ ft., leaves green, 1 ft. long, flowers deep lilac, carried well above the foliage. *H. sieboldiana*, 2 ft., leaves grey-blue, flowers lilac-white, one of the most handsome species. *H. lancifolia tardiflora*, 1 ft., narrow, shining green leaves, flowers lilac-mauve, late September to November. *H. undulata*, 15 in., leaves green with a white central band, wavy edged or spirally twisted, flowers pale lilac; var. *erromena*, 3 ft., leaves rich green, flowers dark lilac. *H. ventricosa*, 2½ ft. long, heart-shaped green leaves, flowers dark lavender.

Ground preparation should include the addition of well-decayed manure and peat if the soil tends to dry out quickly. Mulch annually in spring with compost or manure. Plant in autumn or spring. Keep

moist during dry spells. For pot culture, p in March or April and overwinter in a co frame. Hostas are easily increased by divi ing clumps, preferably when new grow starts in spring. Seed is available of son species; this should be sown in the sprin under glass.

Elaeagnus (el-e-ag-nus)

Hardy deciduous and evergreen decorati shrubs with insignificant, but fragran silver-colored flowers, resembling sma fuchsias.

Plant the deciduous species from Octob to December, and the evergreen species April or September. All thrive in dryish, o dinary soil either in an open, but somewh sheltered position, or against a south west-facing wall.

Grey and silver-leaved plants Every group plants, from trees down to the smallest rock plants, can supply its quota of grey an silver.

Widely used in formal bedding schem are *Centaurea candidissima* and *C. gymno carpa*, together with varieties of *Senec cineraria*, the finest forms of which a

1 Ornamental cabbages are popular with flower arrangers
2 Hostas in variety
3 The red ornamental kale, much used in decorative floral arrangements
4 Ornamental kale, with a pale central area of the leaf

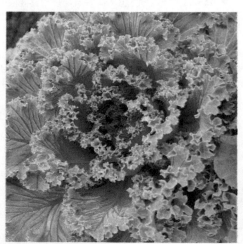

1

"White Diamond", "Ramparts" and "Hoar Frost".

The centaureas are hardy perennials, the senecios sub-shrubs, but all may be treated as half-hardy annuals for bedding pur-

poses, sowing the seed in early spring for planting out in late May or early June.

"White Diamond" and "Ramparts" both have striking foliage, thickly felted with silvery-white. "Hoar Frost" is aptly described by its name and there is a newer and more compact form, "Dwarf Silver", with even brighter and more exciting leaf color than the older varieties.

Two stately silver biennials, both of which top 6 ft. in height, make plants for outstanding architectural beauty for the back of the border, either in groups or as individual plants. The Scots thistle, *Onopordon acanthium*, has leaves that bear a strong resemblance to those of the spiny acanthus, except that they are silvery-white and covered with a fine greyish patina.

This statuesque plant, which is easily raised from seed sown out of doors in May, has stems that are curiously ribbed and flanged and topped with striking grey thistle heads that open to mauve-pink.

3

In their first season plants will make a rosette of leaves at soil level, elongating these into 6 ft. flower stems the following year. Although the Scots thistle dies off after flowering, it will seed itself freely — in the manner of wild thistles — and young plants are likely to appear in unexpected corners of the garden.

This ability to seed freely is one that is shared by the second biennial — that attractive member of the mullein family known as *Verbascum bombyciferum*. The leaves of this plant have the appearance of having been cut out of thick flannel, they are thick and fleecy and are covered with a coarse down. During their first winter grey-white rosettes of leaves provide interest. The fall flower spikes are clustered with butter-yellow flowers partially encased in silver-white fleece.

Grey and silver make an effective contrast in the herbaceous border where groupings of these colors can be used as buffers between others that clash, or to tone down the effect of plants whose colors are too brash or too brilliant for their surroundings. Many, like the silver-grey perennial *Anaphalis triplinervis*, also make first-rate edging plants which, in addition to being completely trouble-free, perform a valuable role as cover-and-smother plants.

This Himalayan perennial is particularly useful for the latter purpose. Plants make compact, silver-grey hummocks whose attraction is in no way diminished when the clusters of papery, white, everlasting flowers begin to appear in July.

Stachys lanata, popularly known as "Lambs' Ears" from the appearance of its down-covered fleshy leaves, is another good cover plant for the edge of the herbaceous or mixed border. It spreads very fast — too fast, perhaps, where space is restricted — and clumps are liable to get straggly and untidy. It is advisable to lift and divide them every other year or so.

Many other grey-leaved perennials serve a dual purpose. *Veronica incana*, for example, as well as forming a silvery carpet at soil level, has delightful flower spikes of violet-blue that act as a perfect foil to the leaves.

Perhaps one of the most useful of all grey-leaved edging plants is the favorite catmint, *Nepeta mussinii*, with its aromatic foliage and long succession of lilac-purple flowers. The common form, about 1½ ft. tall, is dwarfed by the 3 ft. "Six Hills" vari-

4

ety; there is another, *violacea*, whose flowers are a deep violet.

The *Artemisia* species, which include both perennial and shrubby forms, provide a wealth of silver and grey planting material.

The majestic grey-green foliage of the cardoon, *Cynara cardunculus*, has earned it a well-deserved promotion from the kitchen garden to a position of importance at the back of the herbaceous border.

In summer the thick grey stems of the cardoon are topped with large purple thistleheads, very much like a more prickly version of those of the globe artichoke, suitable only in areas with a very long growing season. Another stately grey-leaved 6-footer for the back of the border is the plume poppy, *Macleaya cordata*. Its beautifully lobed, blue-grey leaves are thickly silvered on their undersides. These rather overshadow the feathery, pinkish-buff inflorescences, although the latter are attractive enough to furnish this perennial with its popular name.

We tend to forget that many kinds of dianthus are grey-leaved plants that serve a decorative purpose even when not in flower. "Blue Hills", with purple flowers, "Dubarry", rose-pink, "John Page", cyclamen and "Whitehills", flesh-pink, all

have compact cushions of silver foliage that makes them interesting plants for all seasons.

The hawkweeds, most commonly encountered as lawn weeds, have several species in which silver foliage plays an interesting part. *Hieracium lanatum* is one of the loveliest of silver-leaved perennials whose downy rosettes have a lasting attraction. It grows from 1¾-2 ft. tall but there is also a more compact species, *H. villosum*, suitable for edging or the rock garden, which does not exceed 12 in.

There are many interesting shrubs in the grey and silver category, and as most of them are evergreen — or ever-grey — they retain much of their beauty throughout the year although the color and texture of the foliage tends to deteriorate during winter, particularly in towns and industrial areas.

Lavender must be the most widely-grown of all grey-leaved shrubs. Primarily, however, it is cultivated for its fragrant flower spikes just as rosemary, another shrub with grey-green leaves, is grown mainly for its culinary uses.

"Folgate", with soft lavender flowers and "Hidcote", the deepest of purples, are two fine grey-leaved lavenders for all-round purposes, but where foliage alone is con-

cerned, it would be hard to better *Lavandul vera*, the Dutch lavender, which is notewor thy for its broader silvered leaves.

The co-called cotton lavender has this sil very coloring to a much more marked de gree. *Santolina chamaecyparissus* is the mos distinctives species, its close-packed lea spikes thickly felted with silver. It grows t about 1½-ft., but there is a dwarf variety *nana*, which is better suited for edging th rock garden.

S. neapolitana is taller than either of these its foliage, too, is more finely divided. Lik the lavenders, santolinas are inclined t legginess, but unlike the lavenders, they d not object to hard cutting back and plant can be pruned to within an inch or two o ground level in spring to provide shapel cushions of silver.

The New Zealand members of th senecio genus, relations of the nativ groundsel, include a number of sun-loving silver-leaved shrubs.

Most grey-leaved plants have a prefer ence for light, well-drained soils, but th Sea buckthorn, *Hippophae rhamnoides*, is ex ceptional in thriving even in semi-bog con ditions. This is an attractive looking shru that often attains tree-like dimensions. Th leaves are slender and willow-like an

Elaeagnus can be preserved in glycerine solution. Leaves change to pleasant hues of brown and tan

Many silver leaved plants will dry well and can be used in dried flower arrangements

1 *Elaeagnus pungens aureo-variegata*
2 *Elaeagnus pungens maculata*, will grow to 15 feet. It is a useful shrub
3 *Hosta fortunei marginato-alba*
4 Hostas are useful plants to grow in light shade

female plants have clusters of bright orange berries in autumn.

If we exclude conifers, of which there are many with glaucous or silvery foliage, there are not many silver or grey-leaved trees suitable for the average garden. They could be numbered on the fingers of one hand and the weeping pear, *Pyrus salicifolia pendula* is the most attractive of them all. It is distinguished not only for its unusual silvery leaf coloring and form — unusual, that is, for a member of the pear family, but also for the weeping habit that sets the seal on its elegant appearance.

Although normally silvered only on their undersides, the leaves of the whitebeams, especially when in motion, create an impression of dazzling silvery-white. *Sorbus aria*, the common whitebeam, is one of our most attractive trees.

The species includes a number of outstanding varieties such as *S. a. chrysophylla*, in which the upper surface of the leaves is yellow and *lutescens*, covered with a creamy-white felting. *S. a. pendula*, is an interesting narrow-leaved variety with leaves of silvery-grey.

The lists that follow should form a useful blueprint for anyone wishing to plan a garden or border entirely these unusual and beautiful plants.

Trees *Cedrus atlantica glauca, Populus alba pyramidalis, Pyrus salicifolia pendula, Sorbus aria* varieties.

Shrubs *Amelanchier laevis villosa, Artemisia* species, *Atriplex halimus, Berberis temolaica, Caryopteris clandonensis, Convolvulus cneorum, Eucalyptus* species, *Halimocistus* varieties, *Hebe* species, *Helichrysum* species, *Hippophae rhamnoides, Lavandula* species, *Olearia* species, *Perovskia artiplicifolia, Phlomis* species, *Potentilla fruticosa* varieties, *Romneya* species, *Salix lanata*.

Herbaceous plants *Anaphalis triplinervis, Artemisia* species, *Centaurea* species, *Convolvulus mauritanicus, Cynara cardunculus, Echinops ritro, Eryngium* species, *Helichrysum* species, *Hieracium lanatum, Lychnis coronaria, Macleaya cordata, Onopordon acanthium, Phlomis* species, *Salvia argentea, Santolina* species, *Stachys lanata, Verbascum bombyciferum*.

CHAPTER NINETEEN
GREEN FLOWERS

Green flower arrangements are very popular. Their harmonies are soft and kind. They suit all settings. Yet only comparatively lately have the hybridists given us green flowers. Some of the most striking of these come from bulbs and corms. There are wonderful green lilies listed in catalogues.

Lily hybrids

In recent years the much-improved forms and colors of the highly concerntrated and specialized breeding program of the lily-breeder, Jan de Graaf, of Oregon, has begun to make an impact on the amateur. Hundreds and thousands of crosses between species and the resulting seedling hybrids have now evolved separate hybird strains which are continually being improved upon.

But it is better to err on the side of exposure to full sun than to plant the bulbs in full shade. On very limy soils a really generous supply of organic matter is also essential, and if you have very poor, shallow soil in your garden you may find it better to grow lilies in containers rather than in the open ground.

If you are unable to get bulbs early enough for late summer or autumn planting out of doors, then plant them in the spring, storing them indoors in trays, covering

You can force some kinds of lilies into flower with gentle warmth so that they bloom by Easter

Pot lilies in spring for general summer and autumn flowering. If space is restricted in a greenhouse you can start them off in a cool frame

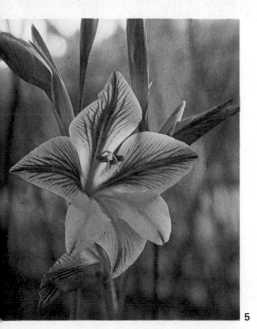

1 The grey-green leaves of
Ballota pseudo-dictamnus
2 Lilium "Green Dragon" is one of
the beautiful modern lilies known
as Olympic Hybrids, bred in
Oregon. It is not difficult
to grow, provided the soil is
well drained
3 *Daphne laureola*, the Spurge
Laurel
4 *Moluccella laevis*, Bells of
Ireland
5 "Christabel" a half-hardy
G. Tristis × *G. virescens*
is characterised
by strong scent

them lightly with moist peat so that their scales and roots remain plump.

Flower arrangers like gladioli which come in such useful shapes! There is the lovely species *G. tristic* as well as green hybrids like the favorite Green Woodpecker. Flowering dates are dependent upon choice of cultivars, time of planting, location, and the season's weather. Gladioli are excellent for introducing height to a herbaceous border, as the foliage is tall even before the spikes emerge. They can also be planted in clumps in their own beds, with the smaller cultivars on the perimeters, or in rows in the vegetable garden for cut-flowers. Their range of color and color combinations is one of the widest in horticulture.

Some tulips are green or have green in their petals, especially the parrot varieties.

Hermodactylus A great favorite, once known as *Iris tuberosa*. Snakeshead iris. A genus similar to bulbous iris, but which originated in the Mediterranean area. Once known as *Iris tuberosa*, *H. tuberosus* grows to 9-12 in. Its flowers are borne singly on upright stems, and are violet, black and green in color. They appear from March to May, according to area.

No special conditions are required but an over-moist site should be avoided. The plant increases naturally but slowly by a spreading habit. It can be divided while dormant or raised from collected seed.

Euphorbia

The spurges, or euphorbias, have great garden value. The include annual, biennial and perennial herbaceous plants, shrubs

5

and trees and succulent plants. The decorative parts are really bracts, often colorful, around the small and inconspicuous flowers.

Hardy *Euphorbia biglandulosa,* 2 ft., yellow, February and March, Greece. *E. cyparissias,* cypress spurge, 1-2 ft., small narrow leaves, small greenish-yellow flowers and yellow, heart-shaped bracts. May. *E. epithymoides,* cushion spurge, 1-1½ ft., rounded heads of golden-yellow bracts, early April to late May, Europe. *E. griffithii,* 1½-2 ft., reddish-orange flowers and bracts, April

and early May, Himalaya. *E. heterophylla,* Mexican fire plant, annual poinsettia, 2 ft., scarlet bracts, annual, North and South America. *E. lathyrus,* caper spurge, 3 ft., large green bracts, biennial. *E. marginata,* snow-on-the-mountain, 2 ft., leaves banded white, bracts white, annual. *E. myrsinites,* trailing, good when sprouting between stones of a dry wall, fleshy stems, blue-grey foliage, bright yellow flowerheads, late winter and spring. *E. pilosa,* 18 in., usually grown in its form *major,* with yellow foliage, turning bronze in autumn,

Europe, north Asia. *E. portlandica,* 9 in. blue-green leaves, yellow bracts, British native. *E. robbiae,* 1½ ft., rosettes of dark green leaves, bracts yellow, good ground cover plant for shade. *E. sikkimensis,* 2-3 ft., young shoots bright red, bracts yellow-green, summer, India. *E. wulfenii,* to 4 ft., nearly 3 ft. across, very handsome almost subshrubby plant, grey-green foliage, yellowgreen flower-heads with black "eyes", spring to summer, Europe.

Hardy species Any good garden soil suits them. *E. wulfenii* prefers a slightly sheltered position, but the others should be given sunny places. The annuals and the biennial, *E. lathyrus,* are easily raised from seed sown out of doors in April where the plants are to flower, thinning the seedlings later. *E. lathyrus* seeds itself freely.

Given time all flower arrangers admire hellebores. A well-drained rich soil is best and although a shaded position is usually recommended, this is not essential, although partial shade is preferable to full sun. Once established, the plants like to be left undisturbed, although they quickly settle down if they are moved in winter with plenty of soil around their roots. Plant in October, November or March, 15 in. apart in groups, preparing the site well and incorporating some manure.

Propagate from seed or by division of roots after flowering.

There are also many delightful annuals, nicotiana, zinnias, African marigolds and the striking *Molucella laevis.* These flowers are also very useful for winter decoration as they dry well. The "flowers" have a papery appearance, are green and look like shells,

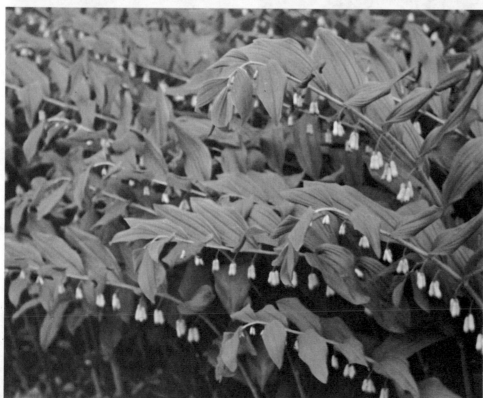

1 *Euphorbia epithymoides* make a colorful spring bedding plant
2 "Green Woodpecker" a gladiolus popular with arrangers
3 *Polygonatum multiforum,* "Solomon's Seal", produces bell-like white flowers in May
4 *Helleborus × nigricors,* a palegreen-flowered hybrid, is slightly perfumed
5 *Euphorbia wulfenii,* is one of the most attractive of narbaceous spurges
6 *Helleborus lividus,* hardy in sheltered spots, has numerous bell-like flowers that turn brown
7 Nicotiana "Lime green" is a modern cultivar, and grows to 2½ ft.

All euphorbias exude a milky latex when the stems are cut. Wash the hands after handling

To ensure that euphorbias and hellebores take water well, stand the stem ends in an inch of boiling water until it cools

hence the name shell flower or bells of Ireland. The flowers are arranged in whorls along the flowering stem.

Species cultivated *M. laevis,* 1½ ft.

Moluccellas do best in a sandy loam soil and a sunny position. They should be treated as half-hardy annuals, sowing the seed in heat in February or March. The seedlings are then pricked off and hardened off, ready for planting out in May.

6

5

7

CHAPTER TWENTY

DECORATIVE SEED HEADS

Many of our garden plants give us double value, for they produce decorative seed heads and fruits as well as flowers or foliage. Some like physalis are grown for these alone.

Cultivation The hardy species require a rich, well-drained soil in a sunny or partially shaded position and should be planted in the spring. The fruits, popularly called "lanterns" (the inflated calyces) can be picked and dried in the autumn. If left out of doors, they become skeletonized. *P. al-*

kekengi grows very vigorously and spreads by means of underground runners. It may be used as a deciduous ground cover plant in sun or semi-shade. Where it is suited it can become something of a nuisance, difficult to eradicate unless every piece of root is removed.

The teasel *Dipsacus sylvestris* is another. Chalky, well-drained soils in open sunny locations are best. Propagation is from seed sown in the open in May or June, the seedlings thinned and later transplanted to their

permanent positions in September for flowering the following year. No staking is required, but the plants need plenty of room and should be set not less than 2 ft apart. The flower heads should be cut with long stems any time in the late autumn.

Lunaria annua needs the standard treatment for biennials, and the final planting positions may be lightly shaded, though they will grow in full sun. Plants make quite large specimens and their lower leaves in particular are large and coarse, so that they should be given ample room. They should be planted at least 1 ft. apart.

You can grow gourds just as you would squash. The small ornamental gourds for indoor decoration belong to the species *Cucurbita pepo*, var. *ovifera*. Seed are either supplied in mixed packets or in particular varieties according to shape. A good mixture produces gourds in the shape of "apples", "pears", "oranges", "hardheads" and other odd shapes. They vary in color from dark green to light yellow and white

1

2

3

Harvest gourds when they are ripe and before frost. Cut each with 1 in. of stem. Lay them in a warm room to complete the ripening process for 2 weeks

Honesty planted among spring flowering bulbs will hide their flowers and foliage when they have faded

Many are beautifully striped, some are heavily warted. The Chinese or turban gourds are small and orange-red in color.

Among the annuals you can find the prettily shaped seed vessels of nigella and poppy.

1 Ornamental gourds produce fruit of widely varying shape and size

2 *Nigella damascena* gets its name Love-in-a-Mist, from the way the leaves surround the flowers

3 *Dipsacus sylvestris,* will grow to 6 ft.

4 The Chinese Lantern plant, *Physalis alkekengi,* has bright orange, air-filled papery calyces

5 A decorative relative of the onion, *Allium albopilosum* is a hardy bulb

6 The papery seed heads of Honesty or Moneywort, *Lunaria annua,* persist through the winter and are useful for decoration

5

4

6

CHAPTER TWENTY ONE

FLOWERS TO DRY

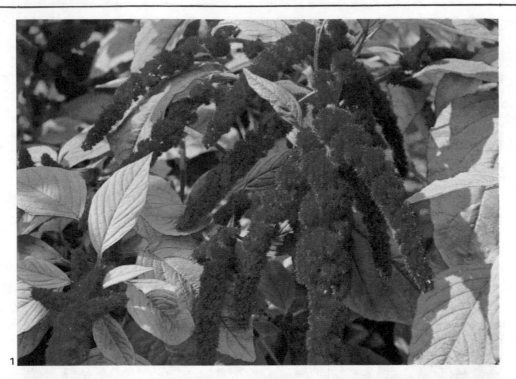

Winter arrangements can be fresh. A good gardener should have plenty of plants which provide a succession of branches, leaves and flowers for arrangements. But even so it helps to have a supply of dried materials on hand. One great advantage of these is that they stand up well in centrally heated atmospheres.

Everlasting flowers

The natural everlasting flowers are those with papery petals, often called immortelles. The most common are helichrysums and other members of the daisy family including helipterum, ammobium, anaphalis and xeranthemum. A packet of seeds can produce a lovely selection. The sea lavenders are often called statice, but belong to the genus *Limonium*, and they include the two annuals, *L. sinuatum*, in various colors and *L. suworowii*, bright rose, and the perennial *L. latifolium*, with tiny blue flowers.

All these plants revel in a hot dry summer. Sow them in the greenhouse in March to get an early start, planting them out in May. Or sow in the open ground in the sunniest spot in the garden in late April and May, thinning the seedlings to 6 in. apart. These flowers for drying need to be cut just as they come to maturity. If they are left

1 *Amaranthus caudatus*, Love-lies-Bleeding, an annual used to provide foliage and flower color in bedding schemes
2 *Achillea filipendulina* "Gold Plate"
3 The silvery-white foliage and chaffy flowers of *Anaphalis nubigena*
4 The purple form of *Gomphrana globosa*, the Globe Amaranth
5 The flowers of *Eryngium oliverianum* are surrounded by blue floral bracts
6 Echinops, a good border plant

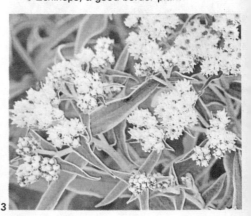

Flowers for drying must be at the right stage of maturity; if too young they will droop and if too old they will lose their colors

Tie flowers into very small bunches and hang in a dark airy location

2 or 3 days too long the petals are less closely folded over one another and they soon shatter once they are completely dry. Cut them all with stems as long as possible, except perhaps the helichrysums, which often have lateral flower buds. These can be snipped off just behind the head and later given false stems. Tie them loosely in small bunches and suspend them from a cord or wire stretched across a garage or spare room or spread them out or wire mesh frames where there is no dampness and no direct sun. The former will encourage rotting and the latter will bleach the color from the flowers. The stems of many flowers bend and are not strong enough to hold the heads. False stems can be made with florist's wire, straws, pipe cleaners or twigs.
Other plants which will dry There are other plants which will retain their color and shape well after drying and which associate

4

5

6

1

well in arrangements with the true immortelles.

Gomphrena

Gomphrena globosa, the globe amaranth, a plant 1-1½ ft. tall, seed of which is available either in mixed colors or in selected colors including orange-yellow, purple, rose and white. There is also a dwarf form *nana*, 6 in. high, of which "Buddy" is a purple-flowered cultivar, and seed of a form with variegated leaves is also offered.

Sow seed in warmth, in spring, and transplant the seedlings to small pots when they are about 1 in. high. Pot as required in a compost of loam, leafmold and well-decayed manure in equal proportions, with a sprinkling of sand added. Water regularly and give a liquid feed weekly until the plants flower, always keeping them as near

the light as possible. Plants will flower between April and September according to the time of sowing. Cut the flowers as soon as they have developed fully and hang them up to dry.

Amaranthus

Both *Amaranthus caudatus*, or love-lies-bleeding and *A. hypochondriacus*, prince's feather, will dry.

They are good for pot culture under glass. *A. caudatus*, love-lies-bleeding, and *A. hypochondriacus*, prince's feather, are two of the hardiest and can be treated as annuals.

Plant out in June in sunny beds. Propagate by seed sown in a temperature of 55-60°F in March. Harden off young plants carefully before planting out.

Delphiniums and larkspurs or annual varieties need to be dried quickly and out of

2

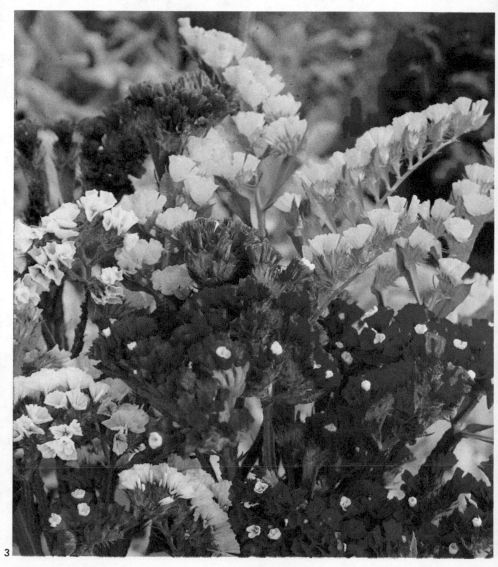

3

Gather catananche or Cupid's dart just before the flowers are fully open. Dry quickly in a dark airy place to keep their color

Some rose buds will dry well. Gather them just as the calyx is beginning to grow away from the petals

ight. An airy cupboard is a good place.

Sow annual varieties in a sunny, open border in April where they are to flower, or in boxes of light soil under glass in March in a temperature of 55°F. Prick out seedlings when large enough to handle and transplant in the open in May. Perennials should be planted out in the spring or autumn in beds of rich, deeply cultivated soil; dwarf varieties are suitable for rock gardens. Feed with liquid fertilizer in the early summer. Propagation of perennial varieties is by cuttings of young shoots in early spring, inserted in sandy soil in pots in a shaded propagating frame, or by seeds sown in the open ground in late spring or under glass in spring.

Achillea filipendulina "Gold Plate", and "Coronation Gold", sea holly (*Eryngium*), thistles, teasels, the lanterns of *Physalis franchetii, Moluccella laevis* (bells of Ireland), echinops, ferns, grasses, gourds, montbretias, cornflowers, heathers, astrantias, lavenders, edelweiss and hops can all be preserved and used, provided they are cut just at the point of maturity. Most of these can be dried in the same way as the true everlasting flowers, or laid on sheets of newspaper away from the sun, dampness or heat for a week or two until they are thoroughly dehydrated. Ferns benefit from pressing between sheets of paper under the carpet, or between sheets of blotting paper under a cool iron.

Drying leaves Leaves to accompany this material can be either copper beech, gathered just before they begin to dry, or green beech once it has assumed its golden autumn color. Put the sprays of leaves into a tall container filled with a mixture of half water and half glycerine, keep them out of direct sunlight until the leaves are silky and then press them between sheets of newspaper.

Some leaves, especially the leathery ones such as holly, magnolia, rubber plant (*Ficus elastica*) and camellia, can be skeletonized by leaving them in a tub of rainwater until the outer parts of the leaves become slimy and can be rubbed away, leaving the framework of the leaf. This needs washing in clean water and drying on paper and can be encouraged to curl without breaking once it is quite dry.

All this material, together with the seedheads of such plants as nigella, columbines, larkspurs, poppies, *Iris foetidissima* (the gladdon iris) with its brilliant orange fruits, honesty (*Lunaria*) which needs to have the outer coats gently removed to reveal the silvery "moons" between, the fluffy seedheads of clematis, the cones of conifers, acorns, nuts and the old female catkins of the alder and other hedgerow or garden material, provides endless scope for dried arrangements for indoor decoration. Materials should be stored in boxes once they have been dried, until they are needed, otherwise they will gather dust and lose their fresh look.

1 *Ammobium alatum*, the Winged Everlasting, is an Australian plant
2 A delphinium border
3 *Limonium sinuatum* is a useful annual to grow for dried flower arrangements
4 Helichrysums provide many gaily colored flowers for winter use

4

CHAPTER TWENTY TWO

Flowers To Cut From Bulbs, Corms and Tubers

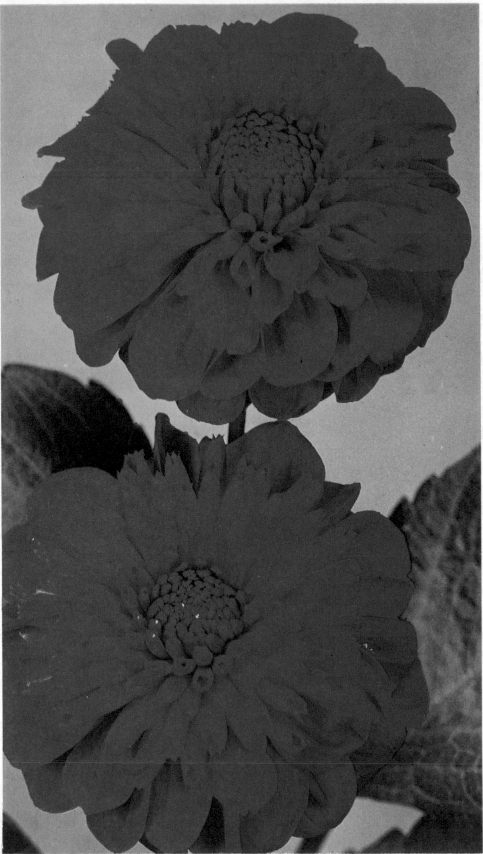

Naturally, what every gardener wants most from a garden is a continuous supply of flowers for cutting, to arrange and to give away.

Cut flowers

One of the greatest joys of a garden is that with a little planning the gardener can have plenty of flowers and foliage for indoor decoration at all times of the year.

Even when done carefully, repeated cutting from the borders robs the garden of much of its decorative value. It is wise to grow plants just for cutting. Any odd corner of the garden can be used for this but the best plan is to grow them in rows in the vegetable garden where they will get plenty of light, and the hoe can be worked around them when the vegetables are hoed. Annuals, perennials, ornamental gourds, grasses and even wild plants can be grown to provide material.

Plants perennials 2—3 ft. apart to allow the plants to develop well and divide the clumps when they get either too congested or bare in the middle. In general they benefit from a spring mulch of compost. Sow annuals in early spring in rows 9 in. apart and thin them to 6—8 in. apart according to the size of the ultimate plant. The thinnings can always be transplanted, either to some other part of the garden or to make another row for cutting. The hardy annuals, such as asters and sweet peas, and perennials treated as annuals, such as antirrhinums, which need special treatment, should not be forgotten.

Biennials are grown from seed sown in rows in May and thinned in the same way

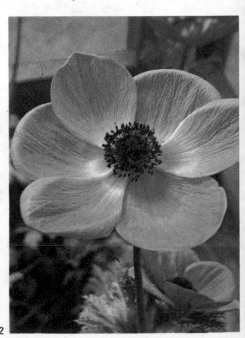

1   2

Wait until daffodils and other narcissi move from the straight "pencil" stage to the "goose neck" development before picking the buds

If you have found that flowers wilt inexplicably after arrangement, try putting them into lukewarm water first to harden them

as annuals, but later in the year the plants are best if they are transplanted. This makes them stockier, less likely to run to early flower, although the flower arranger might enjoy having Siberian wallflowers or honesty in September.

What to grow Try to vary the annuals, biennials and vegetable material and plants for drying each year so that there can be a constant change of design in flower arrangement from year to year as well as from season to season. Seedmen's catalogues provide many ideas and recommendations and usually indicate the new strains of annual flowers which are always worth trying.

If some perennials fail, try others better suited to the position. If pyrethrums, especially the double varieties, give disappointing results change to another variety because some are more tolerant of poor growing conditions.

When to cut A general rule is not to cut material during the heat of the day but to collect it in the early morning or evening. Evening is perhaps the better time, when the flowers can be kept in water in a cool place overnight and arranged the following day. Some material such as *Achillea millefolium* will wilt when cut during the warm part of the day.

Most flowers need to be cut in bud if they are to last. This applies particularly to tulips, daffodils, paeonies, poppies, iris, roses, and many annuals. Kniphofias (red hot pokers), lupins and antirrhinums need cutting before the flowers at the bottom of the spike begin to fade. They will then curl a little in water and continue to be attractive until all the flowers are open, frequently dropping the older flowers; but the flower dropping is considerably reduced if the spikes are taken from the plant early. Lavender, statice, helichrysums and other "everlasting" flowers, grasses and flowering-heads of such plants as cardoon and artichoke need to be cut before they are fully open. They can be dried by hanging them in small bunches upside down in an

1 Dahlia "Comet", an anemone-flowered type
2 The De Caen Anemones make splendid cut flowers
These decorative relatives of the onion 3 *Allium pulchellum*,
and 4 *Allium moly* are hardy bulbs
5 Dahlia "Lady Tweedsmuir", a small-flowered Decorative, with blooms over 4 in. in diameter but not exceeding 6 in.

3

4

5

1

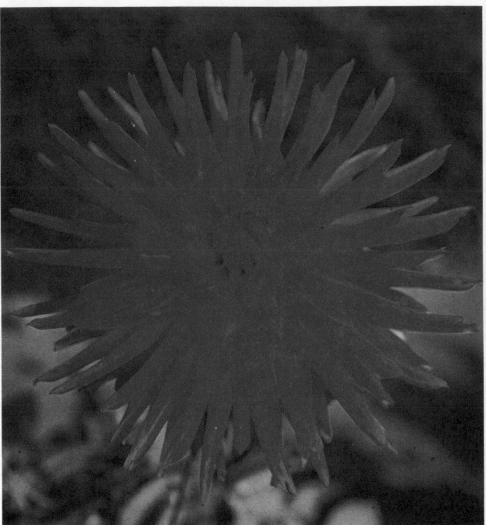

airy, cool shed or garage. If they are dried in the sun they lose their color and become brittle. Often the stems once dried are inadequate and have to be wired or replaced by tougher stems. Seed-heads and skeletons of *Umbelliferae* and the fluffy heads of clematis need little or no drying if collected after flowering, especially if the plants have been well ripened by the weather.

Cutting It is the treatment the plant material receives at the time of cutting that determines whether it is going to last or not in water. Naturally, some flowers do not last well whatever treatment is given and almost no material lasts quite as long once it has been cut as it would if left on the plant.

Always make a good clean cut when taking material from the plant, using scissors or a sharp knife. In a very few instances, for example bergenia and heuchera, the stems should be pulled from the plant. There are special flower cutting scissors which have double blades, the one cutting the stem and the other gripping it at the base. These are extremely useful when one hand is holding aside other plants, for with the one hand the stem can be cut from the plant and carried back to the box or basket in which material is being collected without the bloom falling.

If the weather is particularly warm it is worth taking a bucket of water to the plants and plunging the stems into this as soon as they are cut. This is essential for plants such as bergamot and calthas. Hollow-stemmed plants such as delphiniums should have their stems blocked the moment they are cut and the hand not removed until it is below the water in the bucket.

The tubers of the florists' anemones, *A. coronaria*, which are excellent cut flowers, together with other tuberous species, may

2

3

Flowers may last longer in copper containers, for the copper inhibits bacterial activity

Fresh flowers which have wilted can be quickly revived by placing their cut ends in an inch or two of boiling water, leaving them until cool

4

5

1 "Homespun", a semi-cactus dahlia
2 "Rotterdam", a medium-flowered semi-cactus dahlia which has blooms over 6 in. in diameter
3 *Amaryllis belladonna*, the Belladonna Lily, from South Africa, hardy outdoors in warm places
4 Gladiolus "Weltwunder"
5 The white flowers and golden stamens of *Lilium candidum*

be planted in October and November, or February and March, 3 in. deep, 6 in. apart. Tubers of these may be lifted and stored after their foliage has died down, and kept in a cool place until replanted. Choose a well-drained sheltered spot, previously well manured.

Closely related and just as showy are the Asiatic ranunculus. The Asiatic species need a rich soil. The tubers (usually offered by bulb growers as *Ranunculus asiaticus grandiflorus*, or *R. grandiflora*) are planted "claws" down from October or November until April; those described as "Persian" ranunculus are best planted in late February. All kinds should be planted 2 in. deep and 3–4 in. apart. They are often grown in rows 6 in. apart, for cutting purposes. Apply liquid fertilizer once a week from the time the leaves are seen and water freely if the weather is at all dry. When the flowering season is over the tubers must be dried and stored until planting time again.

The handsome seedheads of *Allium albopilosum* were described elsewhere. There are other species whose flowers are delightful and long lasting. Study a bulb catalogue for these.

Alliums require only ordinary, well-drained garden soil; most thrive in full sun. They may be used in flower borders, shrub border or rock gardens. Plant in October or November, at a depth equal to twice the diameter of the bulbs. Increase in spring by small bulbs or seed planted in gritty soil.

Amaryllis Really gorgeous and somehow so unexpected at the end of summer are these belladonna lilies.

Though these plants are regarded as hardy, the site usually chosen for them is in full sun, the foot of a south-facing wall being ideal. This protection is not essential in mild areas. The soil should be well drained and enriched with leafmold or well-rotted cow manure. Plant bulbs in May, 9 in. deep, 12 in. apart. Established bulbs should be watered freely while in active growth. Bulbs increase naturally and if required for planting elsewhere may be lifted and divided while dormant.

Gladioli We dealt briefly with gladioli in the section on green flowers, so now a little more about these useful blooms.

Some species are occasionally grown as cool greenhouse plants for flowering in March and April. They include *G. alatus*, 1 ft., orchid-flowered, strongly day-scented, scarlet and yellow. *G. blandus*, 1-1½ ft., white, often flushed pink, red lip-markings, unscented. *G. carinatus*, violet and cream, strongly day-scented. *G. grandis*, variable in height, brown or orange flowers, night-scented. *G. tristis*, 1½ ft. creamy-white, night-scented of carnation.

Half-hardy types raised from *G. tristis*, *G. cardinalis* and *G. blandus*, called "Nanus" and "Colvillii", will survive the winter outside in the south and flower in May and June.

Summer-flowering gladioli may be in bloom outdoors from late June until the frosts of October. Two main types are officially recognized: the primulinus hybrids, which have short, slender, but strong and whippy stems, elongated buds, flowers in which the top segment of the perianth regularly forms a hood over the anthers and stigma, airily spaced flowers in "stepladder" fashion with little or no overlapping and a tendency to face outward; and the non-primulinus hybrids, with thicker, longer, straight stems, more bulbous buds set closer together, wide-open flowers facing forward and overlapping to present a gapless ribbon of bloom.

Gladioli will grow in most garden soils, but attention to their specific requirements will be repaid by better spikes and fewer losses. The soil should be neutral or slightly acid, the site must receive full sun for most of the day, the larger-flowering types need plenty of nourishment and continuously available water at the roots, and the corm needs to sit in a fast-draining pocket of light soil or sand. Soils not already fertile should have plenty of manure, garden compost, or balanced fertilizer incorporated. A dusting of bonemeal on top of the soil will help root development.

Planting depth will vary according to the nature of the soil; but on average soils large corms can be covered by 4−5 in. of soil, the medium-size ones by 3 in., and the smalls and cormlets by 1½−2 in. Plant when the soil has warmed up, in late March and throughout April. For later blooms, plant during May. Use a trowel, place a handful of sharp sand into the bottom of the hole, press the corm firmly into this, and sprinkle more sand over the top before returning the soil into the hold. Plant the corms at least 6 in. apart (1 ft. for exhabition purposes) and leave 9 in. between rows.

What a luxury it seems to have lilies to cut! Yet these flowers are quite easy to grow.

Lily bulbs have no outer protective envelope as have tulips and narcissi, the

1 The Golden-rayed Lily, *Lilium auratum*, is sweetly scented
2 The flaring star-shaped flowers of Lilium "Bright Star" are shining white with a golden central star
3 *Galtonia candicans* is a bulbous plant from South Africa
4 The white trumpets of *Lilium regale* is an easy species to grow
5 A popular South African plant, *Ornithogalum lacteum*, is known as the Chincherinchee and is long-lasting when cut

tightly packed scales often serve as a means of multiplying most varieties. Long exposure to air dries the bulbs and insects can get between the scales and damage them. If the bulbs must be kept out of the ground or out of their pots store them in trays, covered

Often pot culture for lilies can be the answer to the problem of difficult soils such as very light sandy types or very heavy clay

All-peat mixtures are especially suited to pot lily culture. In any case some liquid fertilizing should be given during active growth and flowering

3

5

4

with moist peat or a mixture of moist peat and sand.

When preparing the soil out of doors, mix in plenty of compost, leafmold, or other organic matter, plus some well-rotted manure if you can get it, and plenty of porous material to provide sharp drainage.

One method of growing lilies on heavy soils is to make raised beds surrounded with logs. Fill in with a load of sand, and then build up a bed of good organically rich soil on top of the sand.

Refuse to buy bulbs which have had their roots trimmed off because the roots are vital in establishing the bulb quickly.

Stem-rooting types also produce roots above the bulb, but these die when the flowering spikes wither down to ground level. But they largely take over during active growth and flowering. All lilies appreciate monthly liquid fertilizing during their most active above-ground growing period.

Dahlias are wonderful value for money, and so long as you do not intend to exhibit perfect blooms they are simple to grow. They tolerate all soils between the moderately acid and alkaline and for ordinary garden purposes need little or no specialized attention, yet will flower profusely. In their evolution they have produced multiple types and hundreds of thousands of cultivars simply because they are a cross-pollinated plant. This means that it is possible to produce unusual and original cultivars by raising plants from seed, which is an additional asset. Furthermore, with correct culture, plants will flower continuously from July until the first autumn frosts, providing a colorful display over a range of several months.

The dahlia plant itself, which provides a type of stock commonly sold by dahlia nurseries, is formed by rooting dahlia cuttings. Plants grown from cuttings flower later than those grown from tubers, though if you need early flowers before mid-August, it is a good idea to specify on the order sheet "April Delivery". if you have a greenhouse or frame, you can then pot the plants into 5-in. pots and they will grow into fine specimens by planting out time. This is standard technique for large and giant-flowered varieties.

You cannot plant unprotected dahlia plants out of doors until all danger of frost is over. With sheltered situations, free from late spring frosts, you can plant out in late April or early May.

Planting This stage is best tackled by digging a hole in the ground with a small spade. Stakes should be inserted at this time to avoid damage to the tubers which would occur if they were put in later. The hole should be wide enough to prevent cramping and deep enough to allow the upper surfaces of the tubers to be about 2 in. below ground level. Replace the earth on top, shaking the tuber to settle it around the root as you proceed, firming it in. Planting distances are 2 ft. apart for pompons, 2½ ft. for ball dahlias and all others, except the large and giant decoratives, such as cactus and semi-cactus, which should be 3 ft. apart.

Keep the soil watered periodically to start the shoots into growth. Shoots should emerge above the soil within 5 weeks; if not, dig up the tuber and inspect it for decay and slug damage. Slug pellets applied above soil level around the root when planting both tubers and plants are an advisable precaution. Dahlia plants are placed in a hole made with a trowel and their roots set so that the potting soil is just below ground level.

1 The lily-flowered tulip "Dyanito" has reflexed, pointed petals
2 The white-flowered cottage tulip "Carrara"
3 Parrot tulip "Estella Rijnveld", a pink-and-red-flowered variety
4 The turban or Persian Buttercup, *Ranunculus asiaticus*, can be had in a range of bright colors
5 Double tulip "Peach Blossom", a short-stemmed variety